Extended Leave Sub Plans for Art Teachers

Art lessons for grades K through 12
Economy Black & White Edition
By Eric Gibbons

Copy Editing by Paul Rybarczyk

ISBN-13: 978-1-940290-62-1
ISBN-10: 1-940290-62-7

Published by Firehouse Publications: www.FirehousePublications.com
Printed by Createspace

Limited Copyright Agreement: The purchaser of this book, whose name shall appear below, is authorized by their purchase to make copies for the instruction of their students. Should multiple instructors teach from these materials, each instructor must purchase their own copy. This copyright does not extend beyond the individual to a whole department, school, or district. One copy per instructor and their sub may be copied.

If no name appears below, then the following copyright will be in force:
No part of this book may be used or reproduced by any means, graphic, electronic, or mechanical, including photocopying, recording, taping or by any information storage retrieval system without the written permission of the author except in the case of brief quotations embodied in critical articles and reviews.

Printed Name of purchaser: _____

Signature of purchaser: _____

Date of Purchase: ___/___/_____

Venue of purchase _____

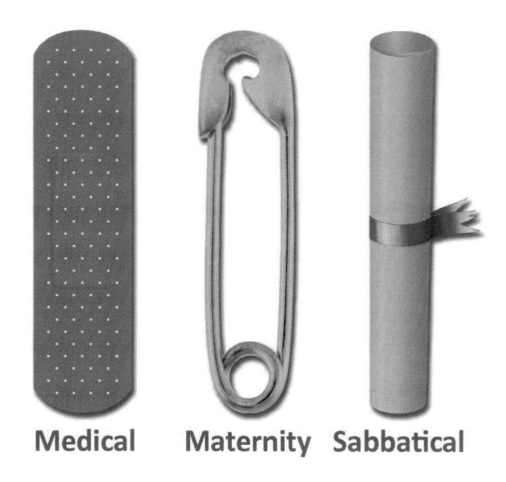

Introduction:

"Stuff Happens" and you need to be covered. If you are having a baby, on sabbatical, need to take an extended medical leave, or deal with a family crisis, you need plans for your substitute. An informal Facebook poll of art teachers show a few interesting facts:

1. Most people take 3 months of leave or less.
2. Only about HALF of the substitutes have an art background or certification.
3. Those who took 1- 8 weeks were less likely to have an art certified substitute.
4. Those who took 4 months or more were more likely to have an art certified substitute.

This book is designed for up to a year of coverage by a non-art specialist with 50 lessons that span kindergarten through 12th grade. Links within lessons will connect with video tutorials. Certified instructors should be allowed more freedom within your classroom. Be clear about what materials you want to be used, and lock up anything you know is too expensive, messy, or special that you have set aside for lessons you have planned for your return.

Many explorations in his book can be done with different kinds of media. As you review the projects, make notes, check what you wish to be used, and cross off items you do not.

Using This Book: You may find it beneficial to cut the binding of this book, and put the pages through a hole puncher so everything can be added into a binder for your substitute. Remove pages for lessons you do not want the substitute to attempt, and set those aside for your own reference. The blank pages within this book are meant to make binding easier.

Things to add to your binder:
Schedule
Seating Charts
Classroom Rules (If you do not like ours)
504/IEP plans
Notes about student health issues
Emergency Evacuation Drill Procedures
Passwords for grade book programs
Map of the room and supply locations
Good resource blogs like ArtEdGuru.com
Contacts in case of a need for help.
Grading rubrics you use (Some options are in the back of this book)

Your contact information should only be included if you wish to be contacted. Keep in mind that you may not want to be distracted by school when you are trying to heal from an operation, or bond with a new baby. The world will not collapse should your replacement not do everything you had planned.

SCHEDULE Periods Classes Locations	1-Mon	2-Tues	3-Wed	4-Thur	5-Fri	6
PD ____ Rm ____						
PD ____ Rm ____						
PD ____ Rm ____						
PD ____ Rm ____						
PD ____ Rm ____						
PD ____ Rm ____						
PD ____ Rm ____						
PD ____ Rm ____						

Student Notes:

Period/Day	Name/Initials	Issue	Note

Passwords:

Grade Program:

Login _____ Password _____

Attendance:

Login _____ Password _____

_____:

Login _____ Password _____

_____:

Login _____ Password _____

_____:

Login _____ Password _____

Emergency Contacts:

For general help with classroom procedures contact:

_____

For discipline issues contact:

_____

For help in planning lessons or using materials contact:

_____

For custodial issues contact:

_____

☐ I will not be available while I am away.

☐ Please only contact me in an emergency.

☐ Contact me any time.

Name : _____

Phone (H) _____ (C) _____

Email _____ @ _____ .com

Notes: _____

Seating Charts & Attendance

Emergency Evacuation Drill Information

Room Map
School Map

Feel free to use these materials:

_____

_____

_____

_____

_____

_____

Please avoid using the following materials:

_____

_____

_____

_____

_____

_____

Things to consider in this room: (Kiln, sinks, storage)

_____

_____

_____

_____

_____

_____

What to do if teachers come to borrow supplies:

_____

_____

_____

_____

_____

Art Class Rules

BE ON TIME...
- It shows respect and responsibility!

STAY IN ASSIGNED SEATS...
- So you can be counted.
- So you don't distract others or yourself from work.
- So you don't get blamed for a mess by someone else at your assigned seat.
- So I can learn your name.

RESPECT:
- For each other
- For the teacher
- For our materials

STAY ON TASK...
- Part of your grade is that you are actively engaged in your work.
- Hard workers do not fail.
- Chatting is fine, but the work must get done.
- Keep your volume low.

FOLLOW DIRECTIONS...
- For safety, good grades, and so that our materials last a long time.

CLEAN UP AFTER YOURSELF...
- I am not your mother, nor your maid, and neither are your classmates.

COMPLETE YOUR WORK...
- A big part of your grade is project work, incomplete projects can make you fail.
- If you need more time, ask to borrow materials.
- Projects must be in before the close of the grades. After that, it's a zero.
- If you have been absent YOU need to find out what you missed.

STAY CREATIVE:
- Be as original as you can, don't copy other work or samples.
- Do your own work, but its okay to ask for a little help.

Cell Phone policy:

_____

_____

_____

_____

_____

_____

How I have handled discipline issues so far:

_____

_____

_____

_____

_____

_____

ASD= Autism Spectrum Disorders

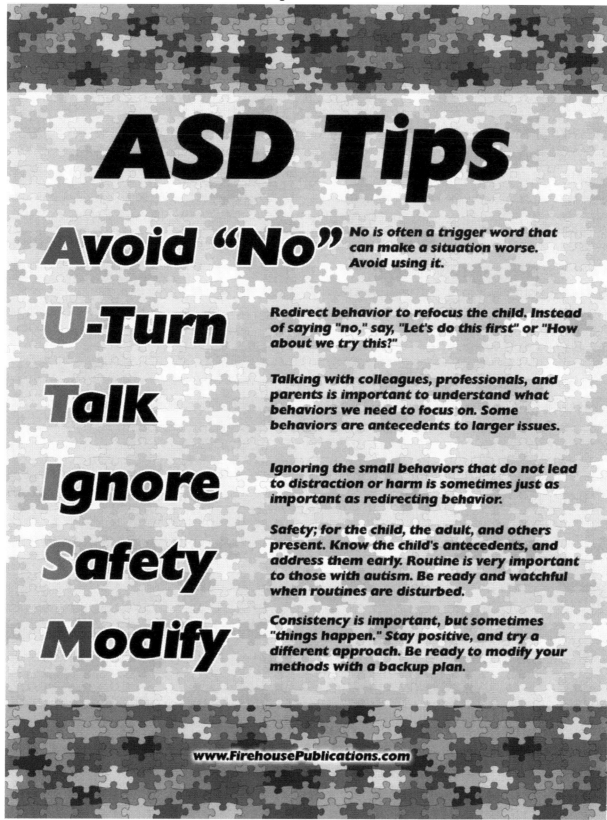

Steps in coloring

Grades K-2 should aim for step 2. Grade 3 to step 3, 4 to 4, and so on.

1 Start with a clean drawing.

2 Give everything a color. Avoid scribbles, be neat.

3 Use intense color where the shadows will go.

4 Use neighboring colors in the highlights and shadows.

5 Use opposite colors in the shadows and erase to make highlights.

6 Add textures and details to finish your work.

www.FirehousePublications.com

Using color and shape expressively

EMOTIONAL COLOR WHEEL

EMOTIONAL VALUES OF SHAPES AND COLORS

There are some symbols in cultures that are the same everywhere. For instance, a puddle of red will be assumed to be blood; this would be the same in New York, China, or the jungles of some far off land. Artists have been using these cultural symbols in their art to hide the meanings of their work or to code them.

COLOR

RED: Associated with blood so it is the most angry color: Rage, hate, danger.

ORANGE: A hot stove, traffic cone, a flame: they are hot you need to remain cautious. Aggressive, hot headed, impulsive, rough.

GOLD: A color of richness and wealth. Also a color of accomplishment. (Like a Gold Award)

YELLOW: like the sun, Playful, warm, enthusiastic, giddy, fun, funny, and child-like.

GREEN: A color of growth. The type of green can indicate freshness: New, youth, students, fresh, healthy.

BLUE: Associated with the sky or water, it is vast, cool, quenching, life-giving, calm, deep, & generally positive.

PURPLE: A deep dark sky, royalty, peaceful, calm, & quiet.

BLACK: A color of mystery or the unknown, also a color of heaviness and depth.

BROWN: Earth, soil, dirt. A color of potential growth, possibilities, a new beginning, or "the end."

WHITE: A color of light, spirituality, cold, and purity.

MIXING: colors will give new meanings and associations, so will using colored patterns. How would you color in your shape to represent your personality?

SHAPE

▲ **TRIANGLES** are associated with SHARP objects like a knife, a sword, broken glass, and spear. They are considered aggressive, dangerous, negative, and unbalanced. Triangles can be drawn in many ways to make them look more or less sharp.

● **CIRCLES** are associated with SOFT objects like a balloon, bubble, or ball. They are considered playful, soft, energetic, positive, and happy.

■ **SQUARES** are associated with constructive ideas like building. They are regular, stable, strong, dependable, and at times, monotonous. Stretching the square into a rectangle can break up the monotony.

Shapes can be combined to make new emotional values. A house shape is like a triangle and a square, so it will be strong and stable, but have a little sharpness to it. What shapes would you combine to represent you?

REMEMBER SHAPES AND COLORS CAN BE COMBINED FOR MIXED EMOTIONAL VALUES. A HEART SHAPE IS A COMBINATION OF CIRCLES AND A TRIANGLE.

MEDIA TECHNIQUES

TECHNIQUE COUNTS!

Neatness is important. When you are neat, it means that you took your time and cared about your work. Rushed work can make a good idea look bad. Take your time, do your best, and ask for help if you need it. What number looks like your work?

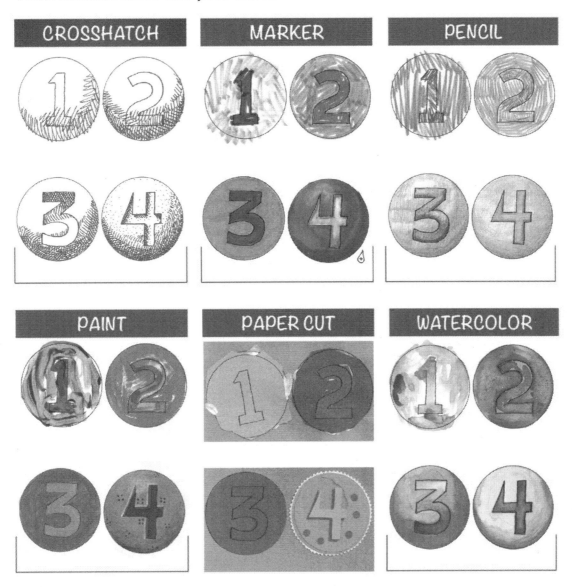

Why Make Art?

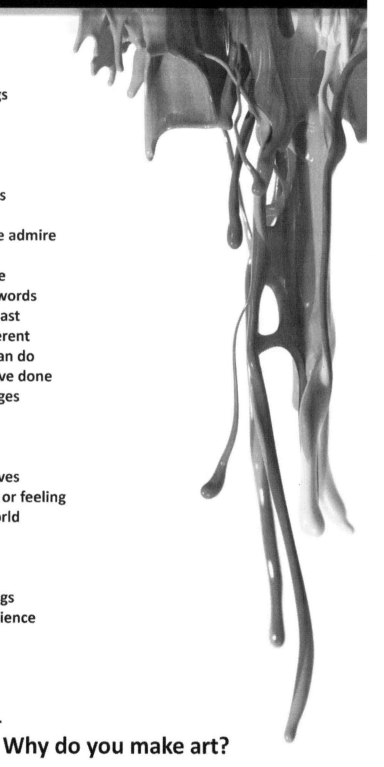

to have fun
to express ourselves
to explore our feelings
to explore our world
to help us learn
to show off
to calm ourselves
to challenge ourselves
to be remembered
to honor someone we admire
to make a gift
to record what we see
to make pictures for words
to connect with the past
to try something different
to explore what we can do
to try what others have done
to teach through images
to empathize
to plan and design
to solve problems
to learn about ourselves
to capture a moment or feeling
to understand the world
to satisfy ourselves
to fill a need
to change the world
to make sense of things
to reflect on an experience
to heal
to appreciate
to tell a story
to make a living
because we want to...

Why do you make art?

START HERE — The Art History Flowchart

Is there a subject? Can you see "stuff" you recognize?	No	Check the title, are you sure there is no subject?	Yes	**Abstract Expressionism**
			No	Start Over
Yes				
Are people wearing togas? (*Roman Robes or capes*) If there are nudes, do they look like the kind you might see in church art?	Yes	Are their poses relaxed or very dramatic?	Relaxed	**Renaissance**
			Dramatic	**Neoclassical**
No				
Is there anything impossible, magical, or "dream-like" happening?	Yes	**Surrealism**		
No				
Is there a strong sense of emotion in the art and do the colors, shapes, or textures help make that stronger? OR does it have a very unusual use of shape, form, color, or texture that almost hides the subject?	Yes	Do you see obvious geometric shapes or shattered images?	Yes	**Cubism**
			No	**Expressionism**
No				
Does it include images from popular culture of regular common stuff with bold color that wouldn't normally be considered art?	Yes	Did it take effort to make?	Yes	**Pop Art**
			No	**Dada**
No				
Does it show very rich or royal people playing or being naughty? Do even the trees and clothes look rich and fluffy?	Yes	**Rococo**		
No				
Is the background very dark but you see dramatic spot-lighting? Is it old fashioned with clothing of the 1600s like from the 3 Musketeers or Pirates of the Caribbean	Yes	**Baroque**		
No				
Is the paint thick and obvious and could it have been painted from observation?	Yes	**Impressionism**		
No				
Do you see hunting, hiking, or farming? (People formally interacting with nature)	Yes	Are the people slaves, or are they looking at us?	Yes	**Realism**
			No	**Romanticism**
No				
Is it dramatic with an old battle on the land, or is nature overwhelming people?	Yes	**Romanticism**		
No				
Does it look like a photograph?	Yes	**Realism**		
No				
It might be a style not on this chart.	www.ArtEdGuru.com			

Supply Information: *YouTube Tutorials Channel https://goo.gl/kbEUsj*

Keep these two things in mind:
1. Return supplies where you found them and keep them organized.
2. Conserve supplies wherever you can. Budgets are tight. When it's gone, it's gone!

 Easy To Use

Pencils should be used lightly and generally erased after images have been inked or re-drawn. They are really good for making shadows and can be blended with a fingertip, tissue, or tortillion. Unless a drawing is supposed to be finished in pencil, it generally should not show much in the final artwork. It does, however, make for a good material for black and white drawings. The pressure on the pencil can make the tone darker or lighter.

 Easy To Use

Color pencils are easy for coloring in and can be layered on top of each other for simple color blending. Young students will be fine with just coloring in, while older students can begin to blend and shade with them. Color should be added in small parallel strokes instead of large scribbles. Demonstrating this will be helpful. The pressure on the pencil can make colors darker or lighter. Test your sharpeners, some color pencils must be sharpened by hand.

 Moderately Easy To Use

Markers and pens present new challenges. Some are permanent and easily stain skin and clothing. It is important that all pens are capped when not in use. Often pencil drawings are traced in pen, like Sharpie or black marker before coloring in. Magic Markers are great for vivid colors but dry out easily if not capped tightly. DO NOT throw old markers out. They can be revived with a little water (10 drops) put into the end cap. Always demonstrate how to color in for students. DO NOT assume all can do so. You can even have a student demonstrate how. Make sure you watch students so younger ones do not "sniff" the markers. Some permanent markers can cause neurological problems. Those will have a strong chemical odor. Water-based markers will have no odor or sometimes smell "fruity."

 Moderately Easy To Use

Crayons are a go-to simple coloring supply for lower grades. This is where they learn to color in neatly and completely using parallel strokes as they get older. Crayons can be overlapped and achieve rather sophisticated results. Always demonstrate their use. (Easy To Use)

Oil Pastels look a lot like crayons except that instead of wax, they use oil. These do not "dry" and improper storage can result in difficult messes. Use rubbing alcohol to clean surfaces. Be watchful for them landing on the floor. One step can grind them into the surface. They are softer than wax and break more easily. Though they can be used at any level with proper demonstrations, they are often used with older students. Oil pastels can be a bridge to painting, as they blend rather smoothly with a tissue or tortillion. For tissue blending, fold the paper 6x in half and blend with a corner. (Challenging to use)

Chalk Pastels and Charcoal are potentially the most "messy" of the drawing supplies and take a fair amount of experience in knowing how to blend, use, store, and work with. They are essentially powder in stick form and rub off on other surfaces easily. Often, they need a surface treatment to stop them from smearing like "fixative." Spray starch is another alternative or clear spray-paint. (Difficult)

More Challenging To Use

Paint comes in many forms. The main concern is that improper set up can end up ruining expensive brushes. **Watercolors** are somewhat easy to use, and because they are water-based, there is less chance to ruin brushes. If you have never seen them used, PLEASE see the video tutorials noted in lessons before beginning. **(Moderately easy to use)**

Tempera paints are a bit more challenging to use. They are water based as well, and if you can't get brushes fully cleaned, they will not be ruined. Some tempera paints look like watercolors that come in dry "cakes." Some come in bottles. They are a great way to bridge into acrylic paints which are more permanent without the potential loss of materials. **(Moderately difficult to use)**

Acrylic Paints are the stuff of nightmares to the inexperienced. If they are not fully cleaned with soap and cold water, all the paint brushes will be ruined. Teachers need to be vigilant about their use. They are far more permanent than other materials and hard to wash out of clothing. **(Difficult to use)**

Oil Paints. DO NOT USE THEM unless you have an extensive art background. Often toxic and require special chemicals to clean. DO NOT use them without permission of the primary instructor. **(Hard to use)**

Painting Tip: Work in groups, label boxes of paint, mix colors on folded copy paper, have cans of water half full on every table. Limit brushes to just one or two each. Let students share materials, and check all supplies before cleaning. Allow 7-10 minutes for clean-up procedures. Organize clean-up teams.

The Three Bucket Clean-up: Setting up 3 buckets for washing brushes can speed things up and catch debris that might go down the sink. Always use cold water for washing brushes (hot water melts the glue that holds brushes together.) Then have students line up and "paint the bottom" of each bucket with their brushes for a slow count of ten. At the end, students should test brushes on a clean piece of paper. 25 students can clean 2 brushes each in about 5 minutes. Monitor cleaning closely.

Scissors are very hard for young students to use, but are an important skill. Be WATCHFUL for those who may want to cut hair, clothing, or worse. Be clear about their use, and take them away from anyone who does not follow your directions. Students can rip paper until they show you they can work safely.

Razors are sometimes found in middle and high school art classrooms. They are often called by the brand name "Exacto-Razors." They are as sharp as surgical instruments and need to be used with the utmost caution. _**If a razor leaves the room, it may be considered a weapon in public school.**_ They should always be signed out and checked for return. See this video: https://goo.gl/NDhcak

Glue should be always used sparingly. One drop spread with a finger is enough to bind two objects. "Just a dot, not a lot," is a great mantra to teach. Even older students tend to use too much. Some teachers like to use "glue sponges." (look it up). Some teachers will have glue sticks that are fairly easy to use. Keep them capped tightly so they don't dry out.

Rubber Cement may be available in some classes. This chemical-based glue should not be used with younger students (under 4th grade) as it can be noxious and difficult to use. The trick is to THINLY coat two surfaces, wait for the glue to dry, then put them together. Always cap rubber cement when it's not in use and keep the room well ventilated. **(Moderately difficult to use)**

Hot glue makes a fairly strong bond and hardens fairly quickly. Before you use a hot glue gun, check out the supply of refill glue sticks. If there is very little, chances are these are only meant for the teacher to use. If there is a ton of it, maybe it is okay to use. Larger glue guns often heat enough to create dangerous burns. Smaller ones can still burn but can operate at lower temperatures. These glue guns need to be plugged in and take about 5 to 10 minutes to fully heat up. They will continue to work for a few minutes after unplugging. Be careful of where they are placed so you do not create a trip hazard. Hot glue is very difficult to remove from clothing and skin, it can create deep burns. Let students know what to do if they get burned. **(Potential burn issues)**

Tape is not hard to use, but there may be precious little of it. Consider what is available and how much you should use, if any at all. Colored tapes should be used only for when it's good for the color to show in the final work. Colored duct tapes are VERY expensive and should not be wasted. Masking tape is great for 3D constructions. Often these are covered later with plaster or paper mache. Scotch tape (clear tape) should be used only when you do not want tape to show. **(Easy to use)**

Clay is challenging. Some clays can be left to air dry and be painted. Air-dry clay can be fairly expensive, so you should be sure you can use it. Some clay must be glazed and fired in a kiln that heats clay to over 1000 degrees posing certain risks. Only a teacher with a background in clay should be using this material. Working with fired clay poses serious health risks you need to become familiar with. Though schools tend to use only non-toxic materials, improperly used ceramic materials can cause serious health issues. **(Hard to use)**

Paper and plaster mache are challenging as well but a great option to clay. Most projects using these materials will need an "armature," a form to cover with the plaster or paper mache mixture. Often this is wadded up newspapers and masking tape, cardboard forms, wire, balloons, or even foil. **Paper mache** is when strips of paper (Like newspaper) are dipped into a slurry (flour and water, glue and water, or paper mache mix) and then applied on top of the armature. This is allowed to dry and can be painted. Wheat based mixes may cause allergy problems with some students. **(Messy material)**

Plaster mache is made from a gauze that is permeated with plaster and then dipped in water to activate and applied to the armature in 2 or 3 layers. Plaster is more difficult to work with and can potentially ruin sinks if hands are washed in the sink. Plaster dust can form a solid rock in pipes that must then be removed and replaced. Always wash hands and tools in buckets of water that are dumped outdoors in a grassy area if possible. Plaster hardens fairly quickly, in 10 or 15 minutes, where paper mache can take days to dry. **(Messy material as well, with risks to plumbing)**

A word about paper. Paper comes in a variety of thicknesses. Paper that is about as thin and flexible as copy paper is best for drawing with pencils, crayons, and markers. Paper thickness is often noted in "pounds." Anything under 50 pounds is considered a dry media drawing paper. Copy paper is great for sketching so as not to use up supplies in the art room. Paper between 50 and 90 pounds is often considered "the good paper" by art teachers, and we pay a premium for that. This is often reserved for higher quality work with oil pastels or work we want to show off for exhibitions. Paper that is 90 to 120 pounds will feel like card stock paper, or the paper for a soft cover book. This paper is good for water-based materials like watercolors, tempera, etc. If your host teacher has paper that is more than 120 pounds, it is their highest quality material and of the highest price. Treat it like gold!

Construction paper often comes in an array of colors. It is important that if you use it, you must conserve even the scraps. If there are scraps larger than a child's fist, they should be saved in a bin for later use. Tiny scraps can be recycled or tossed. Teach children to conserve paper and supplies you cut up. Teach them to cut from the edges. Don't cut a tiny circle in the center of a sheet of paper, cut the circle near a corner. Use the edge of the paper to make squares and triangles. Demonstrate the right and wrong ways to cut or too much paper will be wasted.

Canvas is another material your host teacher may have. Often it comes in the form of canvas boards. These are thick like the cover of a hardcover book. It's expensive and great for acrylics or oil paints. Because of the cost, be sure it is okay to use. Some canvas comes in a roll and needs to be cut up for student use. This sometimes needs to be stretched onto a wooden frame. Stretching canvas is not easy to do and requires special tools. Check with your host teacher about this if you see it.

General Craft Materials: Every room will be different. Every teacher will have something they like to use. Weaving, felting, basketry, macramé, knitting, sewing, and quilting supplies are things you may come across. The list could go on and on. Some of these supplies are cheap, others more expensive. In many cases, these special supplies are used on specific projects your host teacher may have planned. When in doubt, ask. Some of these supplies are particularly enticing to students and may disappear if not well guarded and put out of sight. Theft is always a concern for art teachers. All of our previous suggestions apply. Use these materials sparingly, without waste, saving "scraps" when appropriate, and storing them properly.

PLASTER STRIPS

Plaster becomes hard after it touches water. It is very messy so we need to be sure to be neat when we use it.

1. Cover your table area with paper or plastic. Take off any jewelry.

2. Keep plaster and water far enough away that the water won't accidentally splash, drip, or spill on the plaster.

3. Watch others so you do not have an accident or spill. Several people can work from one bucket.

When plaster has been dipped in water, it must be squeezed through the fingers and put on your project. Plaster will need to be 2 or 3 layers thick to be strong.

If you get water on a plaster strip, use it right away.

Plaster cannot be re-used once it has hardened.

Smooth strips with your hands as you add them. Without smoothing, one layer will not stick to the last and your art can fall apart.

NEVER put plaster water down a sink. Not from your hands, not from the bucket. It will make stones in the pipes and be VERY expensive to repair.
— Wash hands in plaster water first
— Stir plaster in bucket with hands and put it _____
— Let bucket dry and crack out the plaster into garbage

Plaster will come out of clothes, but wearing a smock is good protection.

LIQUID PLASTER

Plaster becomes hard after it touches water. It is very messy so we need to be sure to be neat when we use it.

1. Cover your table area with paper or plastic. Take off any jewelry.

2. Keep plaster and water far enough away that the water won't accidentally splash, drip, or spill on the plaster.

3. Watch others so you do not have an accident or spill. Several people can work from one bucket.

Guess how much liquid plaster you need (cup or bucket). Start with LESS THAN HALF of that with water. Hot water hardens plaster faster than cold water; choose what you need.

Add dry plaster with a dry cup, scoop, or spoon by sprinkling a little at a time. . DO NOT STIR! Too much at once will ruin your plaster. DO NOT STIR! Be sure to sprinkle evenly all around your container so it fills evenly. **DO NOT STIR!**

Slowly add plaster until it makes islands in the water disappear in the water. See picture above. Once you have enough islands—about 50%—**you may stir**. The more you stir, the faster the plaster will harden. *Plaster heats as it dries; be careful if you put it on a person's skin. Thick plaster gets hotter than thin plaster.*

NEVER put plaster down a sink. Not from your hands, not from the bucket. It will form stones in the pipes and be VERY expensive to repair.
— Wash hands in a bucket of water first
— Let bucket dry and crack plaster into the garbage. Toss cups.

Hint: *Acrylic paint or medium can be added to plaster. They make the plaster dry much more slowly. Add 1/10 of acrylic medium to the water **before** adding plaster. This can be a fun way to add plaster icing to food sculptures.*

Razor Blades SAFETY

ALWAYS get permission to use any sharp tools.
— NEVER play with these tools.
— Taking one out of the classroom is ILLEGAL and considered a weapon in school.
— Check that the blade is secure and tight.
— Keep it capped when not in use.
— Protect table when cutting.
— ALWAYS cut away from fingers or body.
— Hold like a pencil for best control.

IF YOU GET A CUT...
— Hold cut tightly closed.
— Tell teacher immediately.
— Wash with running water.
— Pinch closed with paper towel.
— See teacher for band-aid or hall pass to the nurse.

GLUE GUN SAFETY

GLUE GUNS can heat up to about 400 degrees. They will burn deeply.
NEVER touch the tip of a glue gun. EVEN the glue that comes out can burn badly. Use a craft-stick to move the glue if you need to. Glue guns stay hot for a while after being unplugged! A glue gun is NOT A TOY! **IF YOU GET BURNED,** go to a sink quickly and rinse with cool water. If you get a blister, get a pass to the nurse.

50 Art Lessons begin on the next page.

Reminder: Your purchase allows you to make copies for all <u>your</u> students, and the students of your substitute. This book's materials are not to be shared with other instructors unless they too have made a purchase. A purchase can be made at FirehousePublications.com.

Suggested levels: All situations are unique. Some students work at a higher level, some may have little experience and need to work at a more simple level. If students at a lower level excel, look to the next step and see if they can handle the more advanced version. When working with special needs students it may be necessary to simplify lessons by choosing basic versions of the art explorations.

Lower Elementary:
Grades K-2

Elementary:
Grades 3-5

Middle School:
Grades 6-8

High School:
Grades 9-12 (Introductory level classes)

Extension:
To extend a lesson from one day into a week or more.

Advanced Extension:
For students with more experience in art beyond an introductory level.

In general, the younger that students are, the less helpful sketching before working is. As students get into grades 3, 4, and older, sketching is recommended as it helps students organize their ideas, and plan their work. It also helps conserve supplies and minimizes waste. Though it raises the quality of their work is also lengthens the time it takes to complete work. Grading rubrics are in the back of this book for you to copy and use.

1. Forced Abstraction and Cubism

Name _____ **Gr.** ____ **Pd.** ____

Fill this page with 30 lines, and then stare at them. Do you see shapes, animals, plants, or creatures? Trace these things to make them stand out. Color them in.

Lower Elementary:
Have students draw 10 triangles, 10 squares, and 10 circles. Then they trace what they see in the lines revealing images, similar to finding objects in clouds.

Elementary:
Have students draw 30 overlapping shapes. Then they can trace what they see in the lines revealing images. They should color in their work.

Middle School:
Using rulers, have students cover their paper (or canvas) with intersecting lines. About 30 lines that cross the surface should be enough. it should be as random as possible with lines from many directions. Then they can trace what they see in the lines revealing images. This is similar to finding objects in the shapes of clouds.

High School:
Using rulers, have students cover their paper (or canvas) with intersecting lines. About 50 lines that cross the surface should be enough. it should be as random as possible with lines from many directions. Students force a specific image into their lines. It can be a grouping of objects, character from a favorite cartoon, or for a more advanced group, create a self-portrait ONLY using the lines available.

Extension:
To extend this lesson into a week or longer, work done as a sketch can be done more formally as a drawing or a painting. Choose an appropriate media from the materials available to you.

Advanced Extension:
Have students incorporate ideas of color blending within the spaces they are coloring in. Do a demonstration or show a tutorial video to help explain these ideas. Some media tutorials can be found here: https://goo.gl/kbEUsj

Teacher's Notes: _____

_____

_____

_____

2. Observational Drawing Comparison

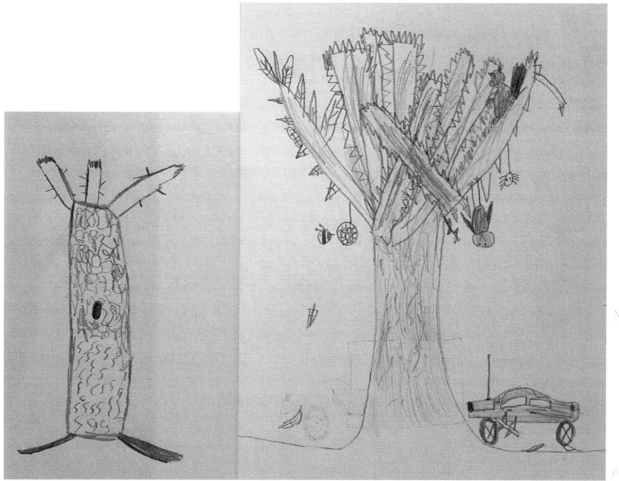

Above: right, from observation.

Name _____ **Gr.** ____ **Pd.** ____

We have all seen a tree before. Draw a tree from your imagination below.

Lower Elementary:
After students sketch a tree from their imagination, project an image of a tree with lots of branches, or take them outside to see a tree. They should do a new drawing of an actual tree. Take time to talk about the differences between the two drawings. How many branches can they count on a real tree and their own?

Elementary:
Same as above, but encourage more detail in their outdoor drawings. Gather students and share successful items they have drawn. Encourage students to continue to add details. If time allows, include a background.

Middle School:
Same as above but ask students to add something hidden within the branches of their trees. These can be actual objects or shapes that the branches make.

High School:
Students should draw both from their imaginations and again from observation. See an example of Salvador Dali's painting "Persistence of Memory." Notice the tree and the unusual look of the image. Students should do a dreamlike image that includes a tree with as much detail as possible.

Extension:
To extend this lesson into a week or longer, work done as a sketch can be done more formally as a drawing or a painting. Choose an appropriate media for the materials available to you. Some tutorials can be found here: goo.gl/kbEUsj

Advanced Extension:
Have students research famous works of art that include a tree. Then they use that as the inspiration for their own work. Not copying, but using the famous work as an inspiration to create their own. Reference real trees as they work.

Teacher's Notes: _____

_____

_____

_____

3. Surrealism

Name _____ **Gr.** _____ **Pd.** _____

Trace your hand below and turn it into an object or animal; but not a turkey!

www.FirehousePublications.com

Lower Elementary:
Students can do this directly on drawing paper, they need not do a sketch first. Show them that the image can be turned in different directions. The 4 fingers pointing down could be legs, the thumb, a neck.

Elementary:
Students should complete a quick sketch. They should do a quick round of "show and tell," sharing what they came up with. Then on new paper do a more detailed version with details like fur, feathers, and other textures.

Middle School:
Students should complete a quick sketch. They should do a quick round of "show and tell," sharing what they came up with. Then on new paper do a more detailed version with details like fur, feathers, and textures. They should include a background as well, showing where the "thing" is and it's environment.

High School:
Students should sketch as above, and focus on realistic details in their creature as well as their background. Students should include additional hands in the background disguised as environmental elements, like trees, bushes, mountains, etc. They can pose their hands in different positions for a variety of shapes.

Extension:
To extend this lesson into a week or longer, work done as a sketch can be done more formally as a drawing or a painting. Choose an appropriate media for the materials available to you. Some tutorials can be found here: goo.gl/kbEUsj

Advanced Alternate:
Have students do a self-portrait, environment, or still life images but let them know that all elements of the drawing must be made by tracing lines of their hands and parts of their hand. A finger used to trace and make an eyebrow, etc.

Teacher's Notes: _____

_____

_____

4. Drawing Popcorn

Name _____ **Gr.** ____ **Pd.** ____

Find a piece of popcorn and enlarge it to fill your paper. Show as many details as you can like folds, rips, cracks, and the corn shell.

Lower Elementary:
Students can do this directly on drawing paper, they need not do a sketch first. Popcorn is a fun choice. 1 bag can provide enough for many classes. After they draw it, they should color it in, and keep adding new popcorn to their drawings.

Elementary:
Students should complete a sketch before working on final paper. They should share their sketch with a neighbor and seek advice on how to improve their work. Then on new paper do a more detailed version with details like cracks, shell, etc.

Middle School:
Same as above, but put the popcorn on white paper (copy paper works fine or a white napkin). Encourage students to color in, add texture, and if time allows, they should draw shadows. Turning off all but one light or using natural light will make shadows stand out more. Showing a tutorial on coloring may be helpful. Some tutorials can be found here: goo.gl/kbEUsj

High School:
Students should sketch as above, working with several kernels of popcorn instead of one at a time. This can be done as a color project, or with black and white media like pencils, charcoal, or pen and ink.

Extension:
Adding more detail, pushing the idea of shadow, working larger are all ideas that can extend this project to a full week.

Advanced Extension:
Students could create their own miniature collections of objects to draw. They could all be glued down to a small piece of cardboard and taken out daily to draw. Encourage the use of a more challenging media like oil pastels or watercolors.

Teacher's Notes: _____

_____

_____

_____

5. Drawing Up-Side-Down

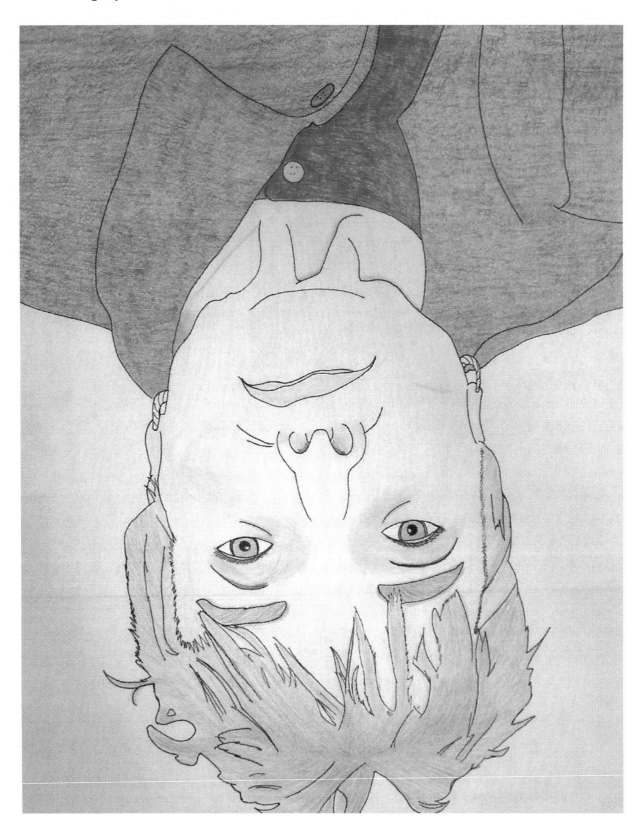

Name _____ **Gr.** ____ **Pd.** ____

Find a face or animal in a magazine or photograph. Turn it up-side-down and draw it up-side-down too. Research shows that this technique is great for developing observational skills. It's like weight-lifting for artists.

Lower Elementary:
Pass out a photo of a face, or images of other teachers in school, and have students draw them up-side-down. Treat it like a game as you demonstrate. Marker may be the best material for this. When done, students can color in. Encourage them to add details like glasses, pony-tails, etc.

Elementary:
Students should complete a sketch before working on final paper. Demonstrate how you would do it. Be playful about it. When done, students can color in.

Middle School:
Same as above including a sketch. Encourage students to take their time to see all the details. Notice how one eye is different than the other. Explain that drawing up-side-down forces us to slow down and see shapes more clearly. Students could be assigned to bring in an image to draw from as part of this project.

High School:
Students should bring in an image of themselves, a family member or person they admire. Have some images available for those that forget. Encourage students to pay attention to details, wrinkles, textures, and patterns.

Extension:
Working large will allow for more detail within their work. Students can be encouraged to color in their work with layered colors. Some tutorials can be found here: https://goo.gl/kbEUsj

Advanced Extension:
Students could incorporate an expressive background once the up-side-down portion is complete. A background that adds an emotional tone to the work, or one that expresses something about the subject in a subtle way.

Teacher's Notes: _____

_____

_____

_____

6. Drawing and Reflections

Name _____ **Gr.** ____ **Pd.** ____

Draw your hand holding an object.

Lower Elementary:
Students can do this directly on drawing paper, without sketching. Have some objects available that students can hold with their non-dominant hand and draw. If time allows, encourage them to color in their work.

Elementary:
Students should complete a sketch before working on final paper. They can use an object in their backpack or one you provide. You could also assign homework to bring in a small object for this drawing assignment.

Middle School:
Students should complete a sketch before working on final paper. Instead of a normal object, provide something with a reflective surface. Small mirrors, spoons, ornaments, or CDs work well. They should draw their hand and the object in as much detail as possible, then add what they see in the mirrored surface.

High School:
Students should sketch as above as a warm-up exercise and also work with a reflective object. This time they should reflect part of their face in the object and draw that as well in as much detail as possible. If time allows, color in work with layered colors. Some tutorials can be found here: https://goo.gl/kbEUsj

Extension:
Students could be given homework to bring in a reflective object. Working large is not necessary as there will be a large amount of detail in the image. 8 x 10 up to 11 x 17 is a good size. Pen and color pencil is a good material for this. Colors can be layered for realism. Adding a background will also extend this project.

Advanced Extension:
Students could create a collection of reflective objects on top of a patterned cloth or shirt. Adding in 1/2 cups of water with objects inside adds a level of difficulty.

Teacher's Notes: _____

_____

_____

7. Tracing & Drawing Leaves

Name _____ **Gr.** ____ **Pd.** ____

Trace a leaf, trace the shadow it makes on your paper. Color in as realistically as you can with shadows too! We will work with one light or just light from windows.

Lower Elementary:
Students or the teacher can gather some leaves from outside. Students pick a leaf as their subject. Before drawing talk with students about the parts of a leaf. Create a list and drawing in the front of the room labeling parts. Then students draw and color their leaf. Tell them to show little flaws like rips or bug bites.

Elementary:
Same as above but students should complete a sketch before working on final paper. Place the leaf on a small sheet of paper. Students trace their leaf and shadows made under their leaf. Turning off all but one light or using natural light will make shadows stand out more. They should take their time to color in as realistically as possible, including flaws they see in the leaf.

Middle School:
Same as above, and allow students to trace, but include a tutorial about coloring in and layering colors to match the colors they see in their leaf. Have students color in shadows with regular pencils and blend those shadows with a tissue. See the pencil tutorial here: https://goo.gl/kbEUsj

High School:
Same as above, but have students choose more than one leaf and overlap them.

Extension:
To extend this lesson make sure sketches are more complete, have students provide feedback to each other about their work, and make suggestions for the final project. Adding more details like veins, and shadows within the leaf will help.

Advanced Extension:
Students should not need to trace, this will make it a bit more challenging. They can also use more leaves and incorporate a stick or other natural elements.

Teacher's Notes: _____

_____

_____

_____

8. If I Was A Robot...

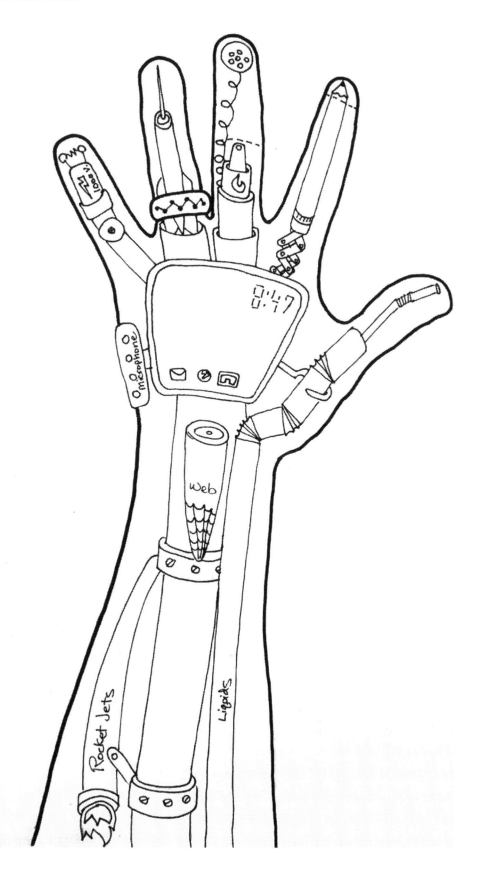

Name _____ Gr. ____ Pd. ____

Trace your hand and draw what might be inside if you were an awesome robot.

Lower Elementary:
Start by creating a list of things students wish they could do if they were a robot. Write this in the front of the room. Trace your hand and draw 2 or 3 things inside as a demonstration. Try not to include too much or they will just copy you. Students can do this directly on drawing paper, without sketching.

Elementary:
Students should complete a sketch before working on final paper. Create a list and do a demo similar to the lower elementary sample above.

Middle School:
Students should complete a sketch before working on final paper. Create a list and do a demo similar to the above sample. Students should consider structure in their work. Just as bones hold our arms in place, what will the robotic frame be?

High School:
Students should complete a list of their own skills, things they do well or wish they could do better. Students then sketch an arm with tools and gizmos they feel would help them be more successful. Students should consider structure in their work. Just as bones hold our arms in place, what will the robotic frame be?

Extension:
Students could work on larger paper to trace their whole arm. If jumbo paper is available, whole bodies can be traced and filled in with robotic parts. This can be done in groups but monitor that work is appropriate.

Advanced Extension:
Students could create a full body drawing of an animal as a robotic creature.

Teacher's Notes: _____

_____

_____

_____

9. Lettering

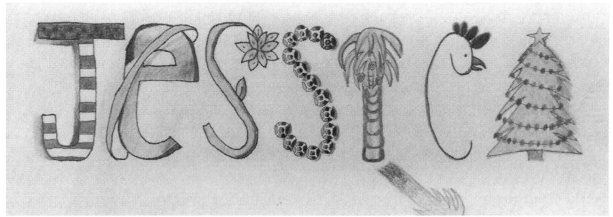

Simple

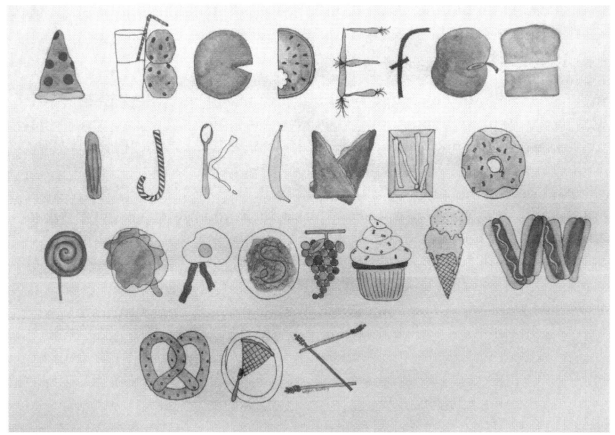

Complex

Name _____ Gr. ____ Pd. ____

Draw your name below but each letter should be show something about your personality or things you like. An "O" might be a baseball, egg, or doughnut.
(If you use your last name, use symbols for your family.)

Lower Elementary:
Students can do this directly on drawing paper, without sketching. Start an example with your own name talking about the things you like. Do only a few letters because students may copy your ideas. If a whole name is challenging, just do initials. Students could build an alphabet as a group project too.

Elementary:
Students should complete a sketch before working on final paper. They should use rulers to make lines on their papers to work on. They should try to stay within their upper and lower line guides. Use the thickness of the ruler to draw lines.

Middle School:
Same as above including a sketch. When making guidelines students should actually measure. Short names can be 4 inches tall and long names should be shorter (3 in.) to fit. Students with very short name should include a last initial.

High School:
Students should sketch as above as a warm-up exercise. They too should use rulers. Instead of first names, they could do their family name and choose symbols of their heritage and things that are true about the family.

Extension:
To extend this project into a week or two, rather than doing a name, do an entire alphabet with a theme. The sample on the previous page is "food." Students choose a theme they have interest in but it should be broad like: Sports, Holidays, Fashion... Some media tutorials can be found here: https://goo.gl/kbEUsj

Advanced Extension:
Working on a whole alphabet but including shades, textures, and details will make it more challenging for advanced students.

Teacher's Notes: _____

_____

_____

_____

10. Writing and Illustrating

Name _____ **Gr.** ____ **Pd.** ____

WRITE YOUR NAME AND A SHORT STATEMENT IN BLOCK LETTERS, MAYBE A POEM OR MEMORY, BUT DO IT WITH YOUR EYES CLOSED. COLOR IN WITH YOUR EYES OPEN.

Lower Elementary:
These students should just learn to write their name in block letters while looking. The tutorial at https://goo.gl/gi8UMb will be helpful. Do an example with your own name. Students can color in their name when they finish.

Elementary:
Students should practice as on a sketch before working on final paper. If students cannot keep their eyes closed while working, see https://goo.gl/K68u5K . When done, students can color in their work (while looking) when they finish.

Middle School:
Same as above including a sketch. When done coloring words, students should add decorations in the margins while looking. These too should be colored in.

High School:
Same as above including a sketch. When done coloring words, students should add decorations in the margins but NOT looking at their hands as they draw. They can look to place their pencil down, but not as they draw. Color everything while looking. Encourage color blending and shading within the image.

Extension:
Working large will allow for more detail within their work. Students can be encouraged to color in their work with layered colors and add patterns to fill in empty areas. Working in pen, but coloring with watercolor paints can also extend this lesson. Some tutorials can be found here: https://goo.gl/kbEUsj

Advanced Extension:
Students could use this blind drawing technique to draw a self-portrait and surround the image with text that is written blind as well. A tutorial for blind portraits is here: https://goo.gl/K68u5K (They do not need a photo.)

Teacher's Notes: _____

_____

_____

_____

11. Combination Images

Image by Rohan Patel grade 3

Name _____ Gr. ____ Pd. ____

Find 2 unrelated objects and create a combination image of this new object. (Like a bug and a trumpet)

Lower Elementary:
Students can do this directly on drawing paper, without sketching. Project or show students 2 objects (or let them choose 2) and draw what they might look like if they were combined. Horse + Snake? Chicken + Deer? Do a quick sample of 2 animals or object, but remove these from their choices or they will copy it.

Elementary:
Students should complete a sketch before working on final paper. Follow suggested directions above. Google Images: https://goo.gl/3RWiZu.

Middle School:
Same as above including a sketch. Show students a selection of these images https://goo.gl/3RWiZu . Students should work from reference images of actual animals (not out of their imagination) then work to combine them. You could use magazine images or print a selection of animals for them to choose from.

High School:
Students should sketch as above as a warm-up exercise. They should follow the directions above, and also include a background to show the environment.

Extension:
Working large will allow for more detail within their work. Students can be encouraged to color in their work with layered colors, textures, and add shadows for realism. Some tutorials can be found here: https://goo.gl/kbEUsj

Advanced Extension:
Students could incorporate an expressive background into their work, or work with a more challenging media like paint on canvas. Working large but with more detail can make this project more challenging.

Teacher's Notes: _____

_____

_____

_____

12. Drawing Experiment

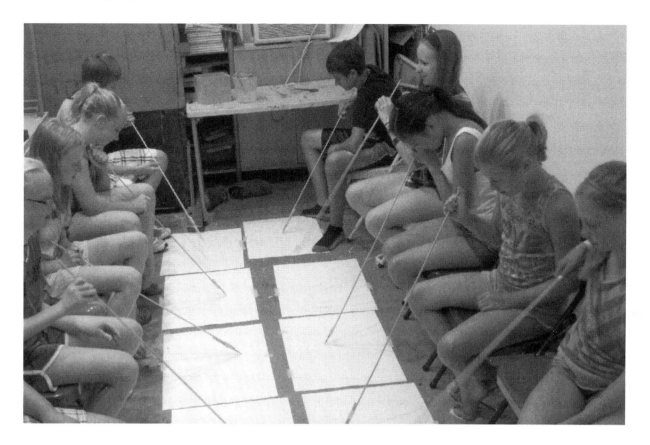

Drawing Experiment:
Attach pencils to the end of dowels or rulers to create drawings.
Students sit across from each other and draw each other.
It may help to tape work to the floor as it tends to slide.

Lower Elementary:
Students can do this directly on drawing paper, without sketching. Have students sit across from each other to draw as on the previous page. Demonstrate how to draw and explain that drawings will look "weird" but they are supposed to.

Elementary:
Same as above. Do a quick demonstration as well. Encourage students to add details that make their partner unique; glasses, pony-tail, freckles…

Middle School:
Same as above. When complete, students should re-draw work with a black marker or Sharpie marker. Then they can add in color.

High School:
Same as above, in addition to Sharpie/Marker students can add textures, patterns, and background elements.

Extension:
Students can work first in pencil, then Sharpie or permanent marker on watercolor paper (thicker paper). Afterward, the work can be colored in with watercolors, pastels, or other media. Some tutorials here: https://goo.gl/kbEUsj

Advanced Extension:
Students could incorporate an expressive background into their image. Something that expresses the personality of their subject. They could also incorporate patterns into large areas of space in their artwork.

Teacher's Notes: _____

_____

_____

_____

_____

13. Expressive Sunsets

Objects within the image carry meaning to the artist so the work becomes more personally expressive. They can write about symbols on the back of their work.

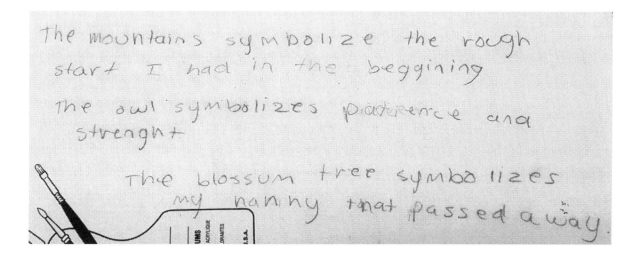

the mountains symbolize the rough start I had in the beggining

The owl symbolizes paterence and strenght

The blossum tree symbolizes my nanny that passed away.

Name _____ Gr. _____ Pd. _____

Sunset Sketch: Create a drawing of a tree with things in or near the tree that symbolize personal experiences you have had. Mountains might mean challenges you faced, an owl might represent a person who gave you wisdom, etc.

Lower Elementary:
Students can do this directly on drawing paper, without sketching. Show them a sunset image (Like the sample here) and write down the colors in their order. Using crayons or simple drawing media, create "ribbons" of color to emulate a sunset. When done they can use black to add a tree with a swing or bird, or other object. Be sure to demonstrate how to lay on colors appropriately.

Elementary:
Same as above. Do a quick demonstration as well. They should put black along the bottom for the ground, then add a tree and something with it they think would be personally expressive; car, bike, swing, person climbing the tree, etc. No more than 3 additional items or the work may become cluttered.

Middle School:
Same as above but if possible, use a more challenging media like oil pastels and blend them with a tissue. See https://goo.gl/QzVgwW . Their ground line should suggest an environment: hills, mountains, etc. Avoid a straight line. They too should use 3 additional self-expressive objects. If they dance, include a dancer…

High School:
Same as above. Using just red, blue, and yellow, they should try to overlap and blend colors. Oil and chalk pastels blend well. Students could cut out objects from magazines, trace them, and fill in with black to make accurate silhouette shapes.

Extension:
Working large will allow for more detail within their work. Students could also do this in watercolor paints for the sunset, and ink to do the black elements.

Advanced Extension:
Students could work in acrylics on canvas if available.

Teacher's Notes: _____

_____

_____

_____

14. Monsters

Blind Monsters:

Students close their eyes, draw a monster, creature, or animal, then color it in as realistically as they can while looking. The contrast of realism to abstract creates a striking image. They could also talk about a fear, then create a friendly monster that would protect them from that fear. Allowing students to choose between the two may be helpful in self-motivation.

Alternate:

Have K-2 students draw monsters, creatures, aliens, and let the high school students color them in with as much detail as possible and return them to the lower elementary students as gifts.

Name _____ **Gr.** ____ **Pd.** ____

Do a drawing of a monster without looking at your hands as you draw. This is called "blind drawing." Think of something that used to scare you when you were younger. If you were afraid of spiders, draw a spider monster, OR do the opposite and draw a friendly monster to protect you from that fear.

Lower Elementary:
Students have a discussion of fears. Create a list on the board. Then students draw a friendly monster that will protect them from that fear. These students should NOT do blind drawings. (See "Alternate" on previous page)

Elementary:
Students should complete a sketch before working on final paper. Follow suggested directions above BUT these students should close their eyes as they draw. See this video on Blind Drawing: https://goo.gl/K68u5K . They should be able to look when they color in their work.

Middle School:
Same as above including a sketch and blind drawing. Students should focus on coloring, blending colors, and including a background to their creature.

High School:
Same as above including a sketch and blind drawing. Students should focus on coloring, blending colors, and including a background to their creature. They can work with different media to blend color better, and work larger than the middle school student did. See the "Alternate" idea on the previous page.

Extension:
Working large will allow for more detail within their work. Students can be encouraged to color in their work with layered colors, textures, and add shadows for realism. Some tutorials can be found here: https://goo.gl/kbEUsj

Advanced Extension:
Pairing older students with the lower elementary students, even K-2 from a neighboring school can be a great collaboration. See "Alternate" on the previous page, or this webpage: https://goo.gl/zdaGHN

Teacher's Notes: _____

_____

_____

_____

15. Blind Portraits

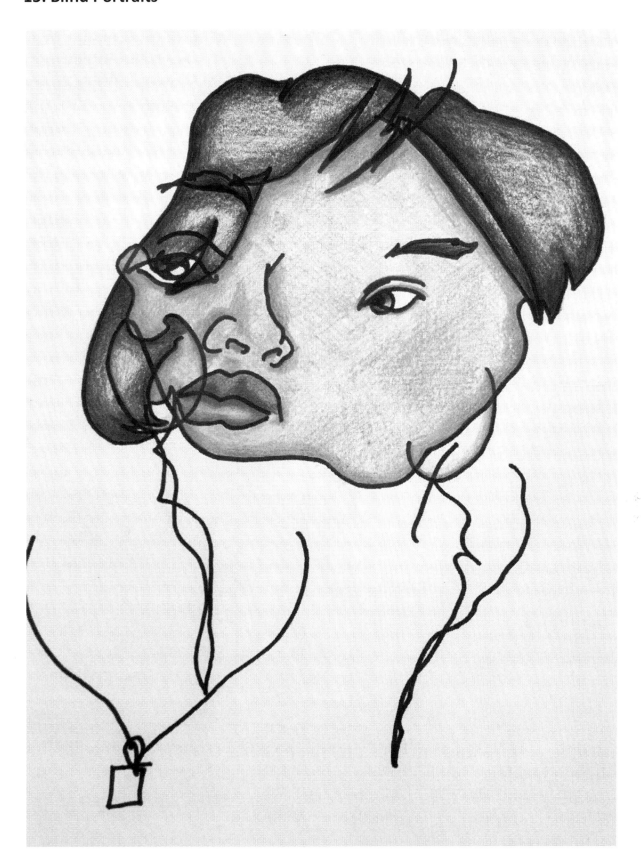

Name _____ **Gr.** ____ **Pd.** ____

Do a drawing of yourself or a peer without looking at your hands as you draw. This is called "blind drawing." It is supposed to look unusual and abstract. Your teacher will show you a video about the technique. https://goo.gl/K68u5K

Lower Elementary:
Students do not have to sketch and should work directly on paper. This video will show you how to do blind drawing https://goo.gl/K68u5K . These students need to have their eyes or hands covered as it is very hard for them not to peek. When complete, they can color in. Students need to look when they color in.

Elementary:
Students should complete a sketch before working on final paper. Follow suggested directions above. See the video on Blind Drawing. They should look when they color in their work and add textures to hair and clothing.

Middle School:
Same as above including a sketch and blind drawing. Students should focus on coloring, blending colors, and shading their work. If someone finishes early, they can create a background as well.

High School:
Same as above including a sketch and blind drawing. Students should focus on coloring, blending colors, and including a background. They can work with different media to blend color better, and work larger than the middle school did.

Extension:
Working large will allow for more detail within their work. Students can be encouraged to color in their work with layered colors, textures, and add shadows for realism. Some tutorials can be found here: https://goo.gl/kbEUsj

Advanced Extension:
Students can do figure drawings as blind drawings and include surrounding objects. Work can be transferred to canvas and be done as a painting.

Teacher's Notes: _____

_____

_____

_____

16. Figure Drawing With Students

Project Resource: https://goo.gl/zK51ii

Name _____ Gr. ____ Pd. ____

Use this paper to sketch a volunteer in class. Start very lightly with a stick-like figure, then add on the volumes of the body and clothing. Try to draw the figure "to scale." That means to pay attention to proportions. Most people are 8 heads high, this means if you measure their head, the whole body will be 8x larger.

Lower Elementary:
Students can do this directly on drawing paper, they need not do a sketch first. Making simple costumes available will make the experience more fun. Have one student stand in a place everyone can see, and have others draw them. This can be repeated with several volunteers until the period is done.

Elementary:
Same as above, but have students do 2 quick drawings, and 2 longer poses. Volunteers should get credit for their work as well. The use of simple props can be very helpful. (Hats, scarf, cape, stick, etc.)

Middle School:
Same as above, with helpful resources here https://goo.gl/zK51ii. Try using different media and after 2 quick sketches, work on a larger drawing with a long pose and encourage detail. Some media tutorials are found here: goo.gl/kbEUsj

High School:
Same as above, students can be asked to bring in props to work with. Students should learn to do "Gesture Drawings." This video will be very helpful: https://goo.gl/JFGLL7 These beginning drawings can be done on copy paper so students can do several in a row for 5 minute poses. Then move to longer studies.

Extension:
Gesture drawing for 1 day, short poses the next, longer poses on the 3rd day, then a full day on a figure adding details after that on the 5th day. Adding color, pattern, textures, etc will extend it even longer. https://goo.gl/NZh5iQ

Advanced Extension:
As above students can work for extended periods of time, but requiring more detail or the use of a more challenging media like watercolor or ink will help.

Teacher's Notes: _____

_____

_____

_____

17. Fashion Unit

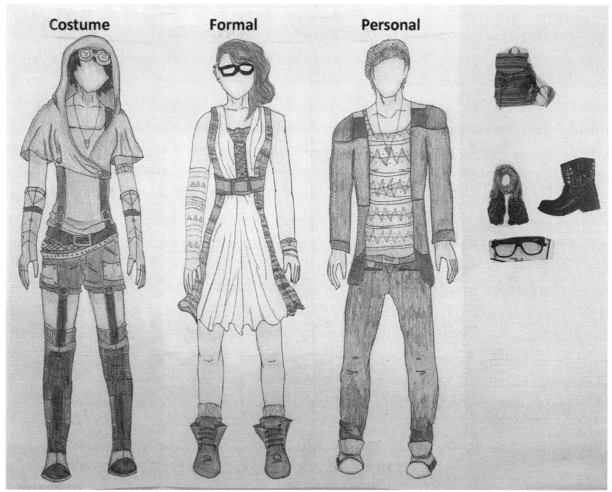

Extra resources here: https://goo.gl/zK51ii

Name _____ Gr. ____ Pd. ____

Design 2 fashion "looks." Choose a costume, or something for a special occasion that would be formal, or something you personally would like to wear.

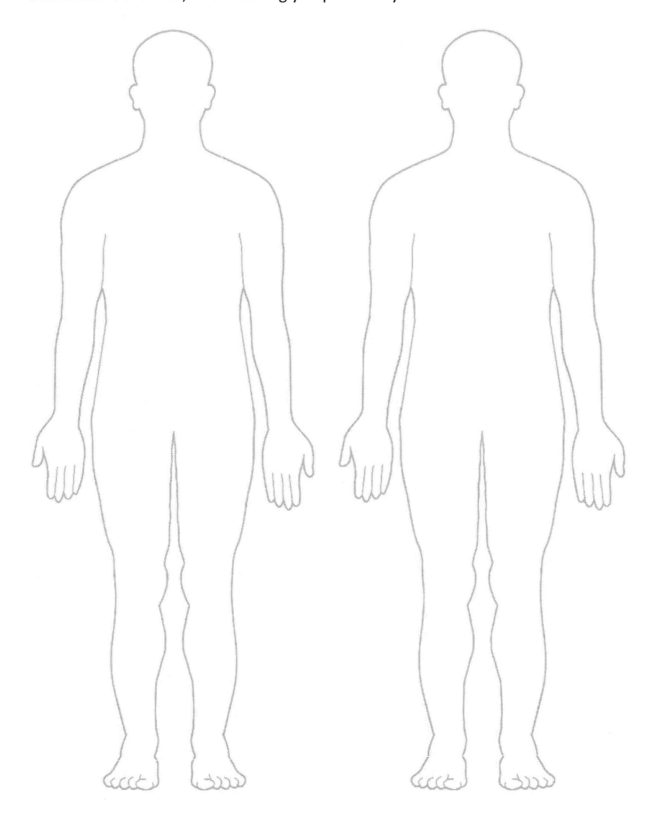

Lower Elementary:
Students can use the sketch paper to draw on the same clothes they are wearing on the first figure, and draw the clothes they wish they could wear on the second figure, picking colors and designs they think would be fun.

Elementary:
Students can use the hand-out and follow those directions to create 2 designs. To extend this, they can re-draw their best idea onto drawing paper.

Middle School:
Same as above, with helpful resource here https://goo.gl/zK51ii . Give students 2 hand-outs each to create all three looks. The extra figure can be used if any of the previous figures are not to their liking.

High School:
Same as above, students should do all three designs, then transfer onto better drawing paper. See here https://goo.gl/zK51ii for detailed information.

Extension:
Coupling this lesson with figure drawing can extend this lesson into 1 or 2 weeks. In the sample, you can see the last panel includes 4 inspiration items cut from magazines. Choosing these first, and requiring students to use colors/designs from their inspiration items can help make the work more cohesive.

Advanced Extension:
Students could sketch, design, and create a design from paper instead of fabric. Possibly focusing on one major item of clothing. "Project Runway" is a good show to preview for ideas and help students get in the mood to create an actual item.

Teacher's Notes: _____

_____

_____

_____

18. What's In the Bag

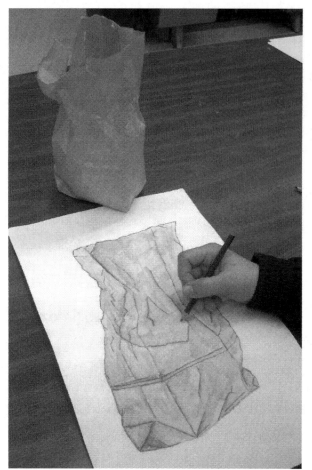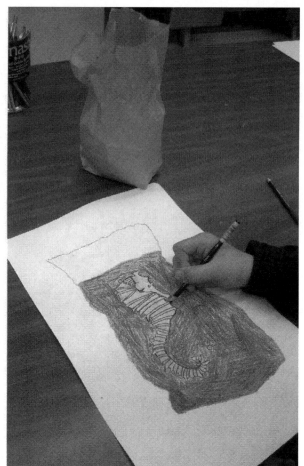

Extra resources here: https://goo.gl/efS8GL

Name _____ Gr. _____ Pd. _____

Do a sketch of a paper bag or container. What is something unexpected that could be hiding inside?

Lower Elementary:
Students can draw directly on thin drawing paper, they need not do a sketch first. Have a simple container (Box/Jar) that they cannot see in. Draw the container. Flip over the paper, draw what might be inside. When the paper is held to light, the inside object can be seen inside the box.

Elementary:
Students should complete a sketch before working on final paper as described above. Before drawing, discuss what are some impossible items that could be in the container. Spider, goldfish, alien?

Middle School:
Similar as above but have students work with a paper bag. This makes it a bit more challenging to draw. Then flip the paper and create the inner object. Work on thinner drawing paper. Some tutorials can be found here: www.goo.gl/kbEUsj

High School:
Students should sketch as above, but crumple the paper bag a little bit. On their final paper, they should color in the bag to make it look more realistic with shadows and highlights. Some tutorials can be found here: www.goo.gl/kbEUsj

Extension:
Adding more detail, pushing the idea of shadow, working larger are all ideas that can extend this project to a full week. Work on thinner paper for this project.

Advanced Extension:
Students could create their own container to draw or bring in something. Then, as above, create the inner object as well.

Teacher's Notes: _____

_____

_____

_____

19. My Opposite Twin

Extra resources here: https://goo.gl/SPZnsa

Helpful Hint: Fold paper in half and draw one face. Then trace in a dark pen like Sharpie. Turn the paper over, put against a window or light box and trace the face again on the other side. Open to reveal 2 mirror images of the same face.

Name _____ **Gr.** ____ **Pd.** ____

We all have time we are wonderful and other times we are not quite so great. Sketch your opposite twin below. They should look like you, just not as nice.

Lower Elementary:
Students can do this directly on drawing paper, they need not do a sketch first. Have students do a drawing of themselves when they are angry. Talk about what colors look angry. How can you show anger? Create a list then let them draw.

Elementary:
Students should complete a sketch before working on final paper. Have a short discussion about how to show anger or evil in an image or a face? (Tattoos, snake-eyes, certain colors...) See the "Helpful Hint" on the example page.

Middle School:
Same as above, using the "Helpful Hint" on the sample page. Students should add more details like textures and colors as they work. Encourage students to blend colors if they can. Some media tutorials can be found here: www.goo.gl/kbEUsj

High School:
Students should sketch and plan as above. They should color and layer colors including shadows and textures to look more realistic.

Extension:
Listing their personal qualities, then listing the opposites to develop a character that would be their evil twin or opposite. This helps the planning of their work so it is more intentional. After sketching, students should share their concept with neighbors for feedback. The class could take some time to do a short critique.

Advanced Extension:
Students could create a painted or drawn self-portrait of their alter ego. It need not be evil, but show off a part of their personality they normally do not share. Color, shape, textures, and decoration should evoke the feelings they wish to express.

Teacher's Notes: _____

_____

_____

_____

20. Compound Words

"Carpool"

Some sample compound words: Carpool, Toadstool, Horseshoe, Housefly, Dragonfly, Football, Hotdog, Rainbow, Waterfall, Groundhog, Butterfly, Fireman, Firefighter, Dog food, Toenail, Jellyfish, Starfish, Catfish, Baseball, Carpet, Honeybee, Hairnet, Hairspray, French fry, French toast, Hummingbird, Pancake, Shoehorn, Boxing ring, Earring, and many more! More here: https://goo.gl/sc034

Name _____ **Gr.** ____ **Pd.** ____

Draw an illustration for a compound word below, but do it in an unexpected way. For example, a butterfly is a bug that likes flowers. What if you drew it as a stick of butter with wings? Carpool could be a car with a pool inside!

Lower Elementary:
Students can do this directly on drawing paper, they need not do a sketch first. Have students help you create a list of compound words. Some are on the sample page for this project. They should write the compound word on the back.

Elementary:
Students should complete a sketch before working on final paper. Follow the directions above and create a list of possible compound words. They should color in their work, add details, and if they have time, consider a background.

Middle School:
Same as above, but encourage students to color in and add textures. These students should also consider a background for where their object exists: kitchen, outdoors, mountains, backyard, etc… For coloring and media tutorials visit here: www.goo.gl/kbEUsj

High School:
Students should sketch as above, and consider a background for their illustration so it has a "sense of place." They should color in, layer colors, include shadows, and add textures for as much realism as possible.

Extension:
Making sure sketches are more detailed will make for better final results. Having students critique sketches and provide feedback too will help. Adding detail, shadows, working larger are all ideas that can extend this project.

Advanced Extension:
Encourage the use of a more challenging media like oil pastels or watercolors. Students could also work larger. Work could be partnered with a lower grade that is covering compound words in their curriculum.

Teacher's Notes: _____

_____

_____

_____

21. Finish The Picture

Name _____ **Gr.** ____ **Pd.** ____

Rip or cut a piece of a picture from a magazine and tape or glue it below. How would you fill this page to finish the picture? Do you want to work realistically, or do something more playful and imaginative?

Lower Elementary:

Pre-rip or cut several images and let students pick from a pile. Tape or glue images down to drawing paper and have students complete the image in a real or silly way. Having 2 examples of your own will be helpful.

Elementary:

Same as above, but encourage more detail and the idea that the image can have a surprise in it. That they can add things that might be silly or impossible too.

Middle School:

Students can get images on their own from magazines you make available. They can create a "sketch" by trying out an image. Have students share their ideas and give feedback about what seemed successful. Encourage students to be playful in their images. Some media tutorials can be found here: www.goo.gl/kbEUsj

High School:

Students should sketch as above, sharing ideas for feedback, and then working on final paper. Backgrounds should be more detailed with overlaps and depth if possible. Work should be colored in and include textures as appropriate.

Extension:

Sharing surreal images by artists such as Salvador Dali or Rene Magritte may be a good motivation, but be sure to preview images as some of their work may not be school appropriate. Again sketch and work on a final image with detail.

Advanced Extension:

Students could work in collage, cutting and pasting images to create a surreal scene. They should begin with a large background image, then cut and paste surreal elements. Examples can be found here: https://goo.gl/opzHMw . If they finish too quickly, these collage works can be the basis for a drawing or painting.

Teacher's Notes: _____

_____

_____

_____

22. Product Design

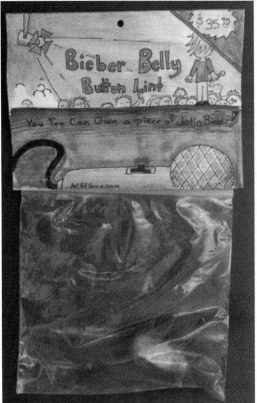

Simple

Complex

Name _____ **Gr.** ____ **Pd.** ____

"Parody" means to make fun of something, but not in a mean way. Think of a product you use or eat. How could you re-design it to make it funny? (Like meat flavored ice cream, bug flavored candy, celebrity toenail clippings, what else?!)

Lower Elementary:
Students can do this directly on drawing paper, they need not do a sketch first. A simple version of this project is to explore silly ice cream flavors. Work with students to create a list, then draw it in a bowl or a cone. Maybe include the student holding it with a silly reaction on their face.

Elementary:
Students should complete a sketch before working on final paper. As above, they can work on a particular theme (like ice cream flavors) or allow them to explore on their own. Start a list with their help, and be sure work is school appropriate.

Middle School:
Students can complete the worksheet and consider ideas for parody products. At this age, they can potentially make a product and the packaging. A simple version is to work on thick paper, create a label, fold it and staple it to a baggie as the example shows. They can include the price and packaging details.

High School:
Students should sketch an idea. They can bring in a product box, disassemble it, and cover it with white paper to re-make the container with a parody product label. See example of cereal box. Make sure work is school appropriate.

Extension:
Taking time to share sketches before working tends to improve work. Coloring with more detail and texture is helpful. If a computer lab is available, some text could be printed and added, like ingredients, warnings, UPC codes, etc.

Advanced Extension:
Students could create an actual product and the packaging it needs to be sold.

Teacher's Notes: _____

_____

_____

_____

23. Self Interests

Name _____ **Gr.** ____ **Pd.** ____

Do a simple drawing of your face, then overlap some symbols and objects that represent what you like or what you enjoy. If you love music, a music note maybe.

Lower Elementary:
Students can do this directly on drawing paper, they need not do a sketch first. Prompt them to draw their faces large and add in a couple personal details like ponytail, glasses, freckles, etc. that make the face uniquely theirs. Then overlap 3 objects to show what they like to eat or toys they like to play with, then color all.

Elementary:
Students should complete a sketch before working on final paper. As above, they should do a simple self-portrait and overlap 4 items to show what they like. They color in and add textures only within the shapes that overlap the face.

Middle School:
Same as above, but students color in the objects outside the face as they would color the object, and where the object is in the face, they color the face/hair, leaving the rest blank. Outlining lines with sharpie or marker will give the image a bold look. Some media tutorials can be found here: www.goo.gl/kbEUsj

High School:
Students should sketch as above, overlapping their face with 5 or 6 objects. Outline everything with Sharpie or marker, then color in the objects outside the face as they would color the object, and where the object is in the face, they color the face/hair, leaving the rest blank. Add texture and shadows within colored area, and if time allows, consider a background.

Extension:
Adding more detail and working larger can extend this project.

Advanced Extension:
Students could use a more challenging media like oil pastels, acrylics, or watercolors. They should critique sketches before working on their final project.

Teacher's Notes: _____

_____

_____

_____

24. Wild Side Sun Glasses (*3D Glasses Recycling*)

Use 3D glasses or make frames from pipe cleaners or wire. Theatres will often donate used 3D glasses if you ask. Spray them with disinfectant before using. Students wishing for extra credit could earn some by getting glasses for you.

Name _____ **Gr.** ____ **Pd.** ____

Turn this page sideways and make these glasses into fun party glasses. Your teacher will let you know what materials are available. Sketch your idea.

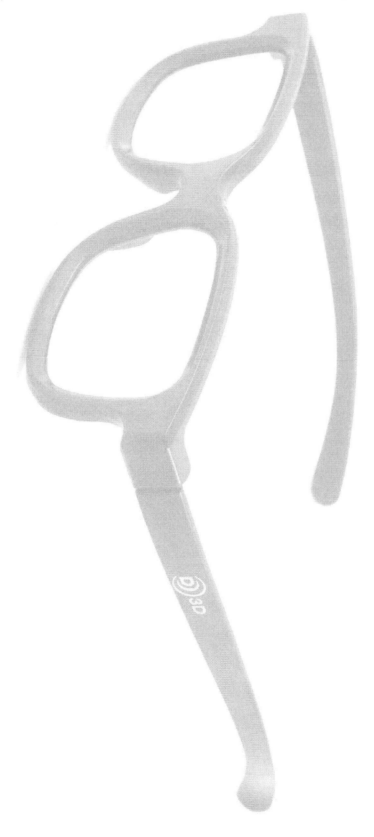

Lower Elementary:
Students do not need to sketch first. Create piles of available materials for students to use to make/decorate glasses. Encourage them to show off their wild-side. See "Teacher's Notes" below for suggested materials.

Elementary:
Students should complete a sketch based on the materials you have available, this way there will be less waste as they build. If they need to make glasses, this may become a 2-day project. See "Teacher's Notes" below for suggested materials.

Middle School:
Same as above, but you could potentially ask students to bring in craft items as well, like silk flowers, craft supplies, feathers, beads, and other decorative items. Work can be more focused if you have them express a specific talent or skill they have through their glasses. See "Teacher's Notes" below for suggested materials.

High School:
Students should make a list of skills they have or things they enjoy. Then design their glasses to show off one or more of these personal aspects through their glasses. Hot glue, if available, may be helpful in attaching objects. See "Teacher's Notes" below for suggested materials.

Extension:
Glasses could be made from recycled materials that students bring in. Hot glue, if available, may be helpful in attaching objects.

Advanced Extension:
Using recycled materials only students build glasses (or crown) to bring attention to an environmental issue. This may require some time doing research. Student could build on 3D glasses, but could also construct their own frames.

Teacher's Notes: _____

_____

_____

_____

25. Cultural Masks

Name _____ **Gr.** ____ **Pd.** ____

What is your cultural background? Are you Irish, Italian, Russian, Nigerian, Chinese? Do you have more than one background? List up to 4 here:

_____, _____, _____, _____.

Draw some things, symbols and animals, that are special to those cultures.

Lower Elementary:
Students can work directly on projects; they need not do a sketch first. Students can use head-shapes paper, paper plates, or available materials to draw a mask that includes United States Symbols. Create a list with student help: Flag, Eagle, Stars, etc. (If this lesson is taught outside the USA, use your cultural symbols.)

Elementary:
Students should complete worksheet before working on personal cultural masks. As above, students can work on a flat paper form, but see "Teacher's Notes" below for other potential media like paper or plaster mache.
https://goo.gl/APZUB3, https://goo.gl/KG3Hk4

Middle School:
Same as above, but students should complete a sketch for a mask before creating one. They should work in 3D with paper or plaster mache. This will take some time, so this is not a good 1-day lesson but rather a week or more. Tutorials on media can be found here: www.goo.gl/APZUB3, www.goo.gl/KG3Hk4, and www.goo.gl/kbEUsj

High School:
Students should sketch as above, and add more significant cultural details. See web addressed media tutorials above.

Extension:
When this lesson is in 3D it will already extend into a week or more.

Advanced Extension:
Students could see some more tutorials on Youtube about more advanced techniques, like from "Gourmet Paper Mache" https://goo.gl/KBX2sY
Most paper mache techniques can also be done with plaster mache as well.

Teacher's Notes: _____

_____

_____

_____

26. Culture Animals and Patterns

Name _____ **Gr.** _____ **Pd.** _____

What is your cultural background? Are you Irish, Italian, Russian, Nigerian, Chinese? Do you have more than one background? List up to 4 here:

_____, _____, _____, _____.

Draw some things, symbols and animals, that are special to those cultures.

Lower Elementary:
Students can work directly on projects; they need not do a sketch first. Create a list of USA symbols with student help: Flag, Eagle, Stars, etc. (If this lesson is taught outside the USA, use your cultural symbols.) Students draw their favorite animal in the middle and surround it with one American symbol repeated.

Elementary:
Students should complete worksheet before working on drawings. In the middle, they draw an animal they feel most aligns with their personality from a country of origin, then create a background of another symbol repeated.

Middle School:
Same as above, and after sketching students should create a light grid on their paper in pencil. (2x2in?) then put their animal in the middle. Use the grid to draw their repeated symbol. Cutting the symbol from thick paper can be used as a template to trace and repeat the pattern more exactly.

High School:
Same as above, including the use of a grid. Students should incorporate more detail, textures, and use rulers to measure their work. Students should blend and layer colors for a more sophisticated look. Tutorials here: www.goo.gl/kbEUsj

Extension:
Computer Lab research time can be helpful. Working in paint, working larger, or using a media that blends well like oil pastels can extend this project.

Advanced Extension:
Students should spend time doing research on their cultures and cultural symbols. They could create an acrylic painting on a shirt or item of clothing using symbols of their cultural background. Be sure plastic is under fabric being painted.

Teacher's Notes: _____

_____

_____

_____

27. Pop-Up Drawings

Small scraps of cardboard or foam can be glued under parts to make them pop-up. Some teachers may have commercial products, like "3D-O's" that do this too.

Name _____ **Gr.** ____ **Pd.** ____

Listen to your teacher's directions and create a sketch of your scene.

Lower Elementary:
Choose an environment to focus on. (Playground, beach, forest, etc.) List things that are in that place. Students make something for that environment on thick paper, color it, and cut it out. These are glued onto a larger paper/poster to create the environment with small pieces of cardboard/foam/etc glued behind them so they pop-out a bit. Scissors tutorial here: https://goo.gl/ymZqQ8

Elementary:
Students should sketch themselves doing their favorite activity. Then transfer just the figure onto thicker paper. Color, cut out figure, add a spacer behind it, and glue it on a background they create showing where they do this activity.

Middle School:
These students could follow the above directions or they could create an underwater environment. Students sketch out an idea and include themselves as a diver or mermaid/merman. Sea creatures and corals can be made to pop out with small pieces of cardboard. Media tutorials can be found here: goo.gl/kbEUsj

High School:
Students draw an environment they wish they could visit. They should include foreground, middle, background, and overlap items in their sketch to show depth. When complete students work on thicker paper to create the basic environment, adding 3D elements with cardboard scraps behind items. See more above.

Extension:
Adding more detail, including more pop-up items, can all extend this project.

Advanced Extension:
Students could use a photographic image of a place they would like to visit as a reference, then re-create it with layers using cardboard behind pop-up parts.

Teacher's Notes: _____

_____

_____

_____

28. Moonscapes With Symbols

Name _____ **Gr.** ____ **Pd.** ____

Write down 6 things that are important to you or that make you unique:

_____, _____, _____,

_____, _____, _____.

Draw a tree and hide symbols for all or some of these things in the branches.

Lower Elementary:
Students can draw directly paper, they need not do a sketch first. Use blue or purple construction paper for a background. Students cut a circle or crescent for a moon and glue it to the background. Then they draw a tree in front with black crayon, oil pastel, or other available media. Students can add swing from the tree, themselves climbing, sitting, or whatever they feel they like to do outdoors.

Elementary:
Students should complete the worksheet/sketch before working on final paper. Similar to above, they can work with construction paper. They could also create the tree with black paper and other outdoor elements, exploring silhouettes.

Middle School:
After completing the worksheet, students trace a circle on their thick paper or canvas for a full moon, painting it in. They paint around the moon in circles with 3 or 4 varying tints of blue to make the sky. When this dries, they can use black to create branches entering the sides of their composition with symbols hidden within the branches. A painting tutorial is here: https://goo.gl/MGS23b

High School:
Same as above, but have students focus on blending tints of white and blue to create their background sky. They can also add a hint of snow in the sky when complete, and maybe some on the moon-facing sides of branches.

Extension:
Adding more detail and pushing the idea of highlights on branches can extend this project further. Media tutorials can be found here: goo.gl/kbEUsj

Advanced Extension:
Students could create a moonlit landscape, including items in the scene that are personally symbolic. Focus on both shadows and highlights.

Teacher's Notes: _____

_____

_____

29. Cultural Suns

Name _____ **Gr.** ____ **Pd.** ____

What is your cultural background? Are you Irish, Italian, Russian, Nigerian, Chinese? Do you have more than one background? List up to 4 here:

_____, _____, _____, _____.

Draw some things, symbols and animals, that are special to those cultures.

Lower Elementary:
Students can work directly on paper without sketching. Help students create a list of USA symbols: Flag, Eagle, Stars, etc. (If this lesson is taught outside the USA, use your cultural symbols.) Students draw a circle on thick drawing paper in the middle with WHITE crayon or oil pastel. (PRESS HARD) Going around the circle, they repeat USA symbols in white (pressing hard). This is painted with watercolors. The wax/oil will magically remain white. See https://goo.gl/2haziy

Elementary:
Students should complete worksheet before working on personal cultural suns. As above, students can work on thick paper, starting with a central circle and working around it with their personal cultural symbols. Avoid using pencil.

Middle School:
Same as above, but students should complete a sketch. Working on larger paper, student can use a compass or template to trace a circle in white oil pastel (preferred) or crayon (pressing hard). Then students add cultural symbols in white. They should organize symbols to have regular repetitions around the edge to create a radial design. Paint projects with watercolors. Media tutorials are found here: www.goo.gl/kbEUsj

High School:
Students should sketch as above, and add more cultural details and complexity to their designs. See web addressed media tutorials above.

Extension:
Working larger or with more detail will extend this into a week or more.

Advanced Extension:
Using drafting tools and rulers, student can plan designs VERY lightly in pencil.

Teacher's Notes: _____

_____

_____

_____

30. Hands & Symbols

Name _____ **Gr.** ____ **Pd.** ____

List 6 things that are important or unique to you.

1. _____

2. _____

3. _____

4. _____

5. _____

6. _____

Lower Elementary:
Students can draw directly on paper, they need not do a sketch first. Talk about things they enjoy and create a list in the classroom. Discuss symbols for each. Students trace their hand and arm then draw a symbol in their hand as if holding it. Then color in. Let students pick 2 primary colors (Red, Blue, Yellow) and overlap to get a third. Close with a discussion of how orange, green, and purple are made.

Elementary:
Students should write and sketch before working on final paper. See above for discussion. Have students trace their hand and arm twice, overlapping to make an "X." Put a symbol in each hand. Color with only primary colors, overlapping to make mixes. Discuss the different color mixes and how they were created.

Middle School:
Students should write and sketch before working on final paper. See above for discussions. Have students trace their hand and arm four times, overlapping like the example. Put a symbol in each hand. Color with only primary colors, overlapping to make mixes. Students may also use black and white within mixes. This can be done as a drawing or painting. Some tutorials are here: goo.gl/kbEUsj

High School:
Students should sketch as above, but should work with watercolor or acrylic paints. Images should be outlined in black Sharpie or permanent marker, then re-traced at the end. Pattern can be added to large areas. www.goo.gl/RWt5sa

Extension:
As a painting, this will take more than a week, from sketching to final image.

Advanced Extension:
Overlapping hands, and designating each as a primary color, can make this into a more intense color theory exploration. See https://goo.gl/RWt5sa

Teacher's Notes: _____

_____

_____

31. Wire Food and Hunger Unit

Name _____ Gr. ____ Pd. ____

A continuous line drawing is like an Etch-a-sketch game. When we draw we usually lift our pencils often. Do a drawing below of your favorite meal, include the plate, drink, and utensils, but draw each item with one continuous line.

Write a fact about local, state, US, or global hunger below: _____

_____

_____

Lower Elementary:
Without sketching, have students create items of food from pipe cleaners or other soft wire. These can be glued to a paper plate. Have a discussion about hunger and create a bulletin board about a hunger issue and display artwork.

Elementary:
Have students complete the worksheet to generate ideas. If they are unable to access the internet, have hunger facts in a bucket for them to pick from. Using soft wire, students create a place setting and write a hunger fact on the plate or the placemat. Display in the school lunchroom or library. If possible collect non-perishable items for a local charity or food pantry.

Middle School:
Same as above, if possible, allow students to research facts. They should list them so facts are not repeated. Students should also create eating utensils. Work can be displayed on a paper plate and placemat with their fact on the border. Use rulers to draw a border as in the example work.

High School:
Students should sketch as above, encourage more detail, utensils, drinks, and other items for the table like salt and pepper, candles, etc. then display artwork.

Extension:
Adding more detail, using lettering templates for the facts, working on a larger school display, and coordinating with a local food bank can add to this project.

Advanced Extension:
Students could be paired with their peers to create additional items for a display that would be more challenging. Decorative cake, candelabra, serving dishes, etc. This could be done as a school-wide service project across multiple grade levels.

Teacher's Notes: _____

_____

_____

_____

32. Inside-Outside/Front-Back

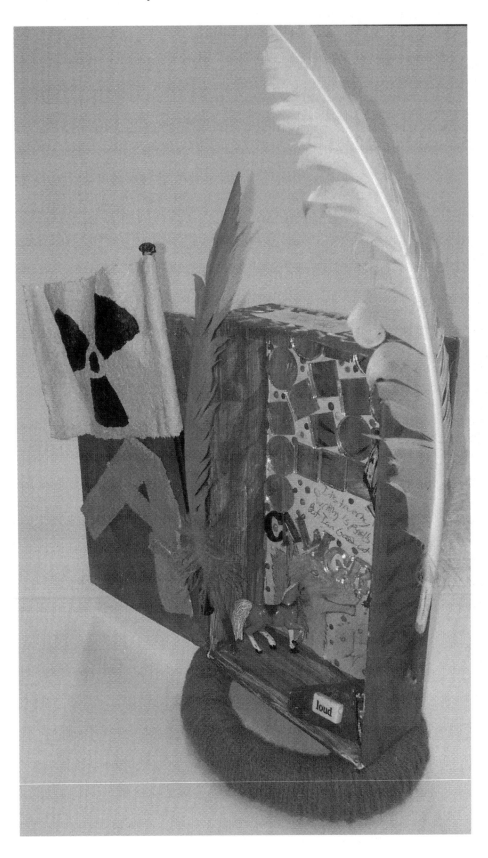

Name _____ **Gr.** ____ **Pd.** ____

Below is a box. Put things in the box to show what is important to you and the talents you have. Outside the box draw symbols and things that represent what others think they know about you. Some things might not be true about you.

Lower Elementary:
Students can do this directly on drawing paper without sketching. Fold paper like a book in half. On the cover, draw what people think they know about you, inside, draw what people only know about you when you are friends. Create a list to get students thinking/talking about these things and why they might be different.

Elementary:
Similar to above, but students should sketch on plain copy paper after folding in half like a book. Have a discussion about sketches, then create a list to generate more ideas. Discuss bullying and how some students are "judged by their covers."

Middle School:
If students can bring in boxes and work 3D then they should complete the handout. If they must work flat, follow above directions but require 4 symbols on the front and 4 more inside. Media tutorials can be found here: goo.gl/kbEUsj

High School:
Students should sketch as above, working in either 2D or 3D. Use more symbols for the back and front of the project, and filling the inside with scenes and images.

Extension:
Having students build their own boxes will add to this project, as well as incorporating recycling by having students bring in items as "homework."

Advanced Extension:
Students should use all white materials on the inside of their box, and all white or black materials for the outside. They can cut, paste, texture, and fold black and white paper to create symbolic items to represent their inner personality, and the one other perceive them to be. Alternately, the outside could be the personality they project to other people.

Teacher's Notes: _____

_____

_____

_____

33. Famous Quote Illustration

Name _____ **Gr.** ____ **Pd.** ____

Write a famous quote about art below, and decorate it to show off the meaning.

Lower Elementary:
Students can draw directly on drawing paper. Post a famous yet simple quote about art. Have students write it in the middle of their papers. Discuss what the quote might mean. Students decorate around the quote to show off the meaning.
"Every child is an artist, the problem is staying an artist when you grow up" ~ Pablo Picasso

Elementary:
Students should complete a sketch before working on final paper. They should work on one quote as above, or pick from quotes you provide. Some quotes can be found here: https://goo.gl/JSrvuy and more here: https://goo.gl/vjmjEM

Middle School:
Same as above, but if students are able, they should research quotes and record them for their project. A list too can be provided based on the above-cited webpages. Each student should have a unique quote. Some media tutorials can be found here: goo.gl/kbEUsj and this project is detailed here: www.goo.gl/JSrvuy

High School:
Students should sketch work as detailed above. They should include more detail, and with a more challenging media like oil pastels or watercolors.

Extension:
Students could do a day of research for this project, then another to work on a sketch before creating their illustration. Having students work in a broad selection of media can result in more diverse results.

Advanced Extension:
Students could research a stanza of a poem or quote to create a more detailed illustration. They could incorporate depth into their work by having overlaps, foreground, middle-ground, and background elements.

Teacher's Notes: _____

_____

_____

_____

34. Idioms

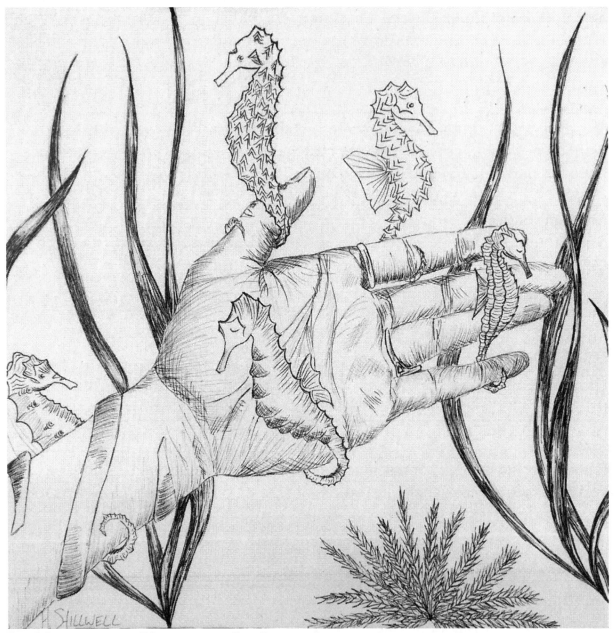

"Hold Your Horses" by Hope Stillwell a student teacher at the time.

Cross Hatching Tutorial here: https://goo.gl/1uG2kn
Many idioms available here: https://goo.gl/Z4E3HM

Name _____ **Gr.** ____ **Pd.** ____

Draw an illustration for an idiom below, but do it in an unexpected way. For example, "hold your horses" means to be patient. You could draw it as a hand holding some seahorses.

Lower Elementary:
Students can do this directly on drawing paper, they need not do a sketch first. Post a few idioms and discuss their meaning. One is on the sample page for this project. Then they can draw directly, writing the idiom on the back of their paper.

Elementary:
Students should complete a sketch before working on final paper. Either post some idioms to discuss and work from, or have them pick idioms from a hat. Have them color in neatly. Media tutorials are here: www.goo.gl/kbEUsj

Middle School:
Same as above, but encourage students to color in and add textures. These students should also consider a background for where their illustration exists: kitchen, outdoors, mountains, backyard, etc…

High School:
Students should sketch as above, and consider a background for their illustration so it has a "sense of place." They should color in, layer colors, include shadows, and add textures for as much realism as possible.

Extension:
Making sure sketches are more detailed will make for better final results. Having students critique sketches and provide feedback too will help. Adding detail, shadows, working larger are all ideas that can extend this project.

Advanced Extension:
Students could explore/research idioms from other cultures, or their own heritage. The final image may include text in an artistic way. Doing this in a more challenging media will also be more interesting for these students.

Teacher's Notes: _____

_____

_____

_____

35. Expressive Silhouettes

Lesson and resources here: https://goo.gl/4gXbSr
Video here: https://goo.gl/RhrTC5

Name _____ **Gr.** ____ **Pd.** ____

Inside the face draw shapes, lines, textures, patterns, symbols, and use colors that show what you feel/know about yourself. The outside should show how you feel about the world or your future. Try to keep your work abstract and symbolic.

Lower Elementary:
Students do not need to sketch. They should draw a large circle/oval on their paper. Inside they draw the things they do best and enjoy. Outside draw the things they hope to do or things they when they grow up.

Elementary:
Students should complete the worksheet and sketch. They should share their sketch with a neighbor and seek advice on how to improve their work. Then on new paper do a more detailed version. Faces can be traced on final paper with the use of a projector, or a large template can be made and traced.

Middle School:
Same as above, but encourage students to color in, add texture, patterns. Show them the example image for some inspiration. Trace faces on final paper by projecting shadows. Some tutorials can be found here: www.goo.gl/kbEUsj

High School:
Students should sketch as above, and work more symbolically. They should avoid overt concrete images like hearts, peace signs, and objects. This poster will be helpful in working more abstractly and symbolically: https://goo.gl/GwpmcJ

Extension:
The example image was done in pencil, then retraced in permanent pen (Sharpie), and then colored with watercolors. This took a bit more than a week to complete. Working larger or encouraging more detail can help extend this project.

Advanced Extension:
Students could create this project as a sculpture, creating a head that opens and juxtaposing images inside and outside the head form. Creating a large acrylic painting after sketching elevates the level of difficulty.

Teacher's Notes: _____

_____

_____

_____

36. Black & White

Note: The black is construction paper that was glued onto white drawing paper. Though these lines were made by ripping paper and gluing vertically, this can be done in many different ways. You could put one stripe of black down the middle, one shape in the middle, several crisscross stripes, etc.

In this example, spray glue was used, but white school glue, glue stick, rubber cement, all will work as well. Water-based glues tend to curl the paper.

Name _____ **Gr.** ____ **Pd.** ____

Glue a piece of black construction paper below. It can be a large shape, or a stripe of black going down the middle. (Follow your teacher's instructions.)

Lower Elementary:
Students can work directly on their final paper. A simple version of this project would be to glue half a sheet of black paper onto white and have students draw themselves on both sides. The dark side would be their night activities and the light side what they do during the day. Construction paper crayons work best for this, but test what you have available and see if it will work on black.

Elementary:
Students can also work on final paper, gluing down 1, 2, or 3 shapes of black or stripes of black paper on their drawing paper. Create a collection of objects for them to draw, or they could draw each other. Test media to be sure it works on black as well as white. Oil pastel may be a good choice but can be messy.

Middle School:
Depending on time constraints, students can sketch to get the feeling of a new material. Same directions as above, but encourage students to color in, add texture, and if time allows, they should draw shadows. Showing a tutorial on coloring may be helpful. Some tutorials can be found here: goo.gl/kbEUsj

High School:
Students should sketch as above, blending and layering colors, and including a background or the surroundings. Students can alter colors on the black portions.

Extension:
Students could work with complementary colors (opposites) in the black areas and normal colors in white areas. Still-life objects can be gathered from student backpacks, or brought in for homework. Encourage more detail than other grades.

Advanced Extension:
Students could make their own still life collections and/or work from photos they take. They can work with black as well as other bold colors.

Teacher's Notes: _____

_____

_____

37. If I Were President...

Enlarge the image on the next page to 11 x 17 inch paper if possible. The bill has been altered so that it cannot be mistaken as currency. The page can also be used to sketch work before going onto the final paper.

Name _____ Gr. ____ Pd. ____

Draw yourself as president on this fake one-hundred dollar bill.

Lower Elementary:
Students can draw on the handout, but to extend this lesson, they could draw themselves as if they were the President, doing something "Presidential." Discuss what a President might wear and do before drawing. Create a list.

Elementary:
Students should complete a sketch before working on final paper. They should share their sketch with a neighbor and seek advice on how to improve their work. If possible, hand feed 11 x 17 paper through a copier to make drawing paper.

Middle School:
Same as above, but these students may be able to design their own bill with a decorative border and monetary amount. Students should use rulers to plan their work. It may be helpful to have an oval template to trace.

High School:
Students should sketch as above, depending on time available, students could design and create their own bill. Some tutorials can be found here: goo.gl/kbEUsj

Extension:
Working from scratch, and creating their own bill will extend this lesson. Students could design the front and back of the bill, putting an image of an important event, or their own home on the back as many US bills have. If a Spirograph is available this may be helpful in making geometric designs.

Advanced Extension:
Students could create a coin by carving into plaster discs or making coins from clay. This video may provide some perspective https://goo.gl/bTnjZN
Students could also design a bill digitally if those resources are available.

Teacher's Notes: _____

_____

_____

_____

38. This is what I Like

This is based on Giuseppe Arcimboldo's art. Samples here: https://goo.gl/KDmLBV

Name _____ **Gr.** ____ **Pd.** ____

Create a self-portrait below, but draw all the parts from the foods, toys, games, and characters you enjoy. You can include symbols, too, of your personality.

Lower Elementary:
Students can draw directly on paper without sketching. Show students samples of Giuseppe Arcimboldo's art. Samples here: https://goo.gl/KDmLBV The parts of the face should be drawn with the foods, toys, games that the students enjoy. Teacher could make a sample with student input.

Elementary:
Students should complete a sketch before working on final paper. They should share their sketch with a neighbor and seek advice on how to improve their work. Then on final paper do a more detailed version.

Middle School:
Same as above, but working larger or with a more challenging drawing media. Some tutorials can be found here: goo.gl/kbEUsj

High School:
Students should sketch as above, and make the background of their image somewhere they would like to be instead of school. They should focus on details, textures, patterns, and morphing images to look more like facial features. Their final piece can be larger than lower grades or in a more challenging media.

Extension:
Working this as a sketch for a painting project will extend this. Adding shadows, color blends, and detailed textures will also extend the project.

Advanced Extension:
Students could essentially do the same project but be required to use resource images for all their elements. For example, if the nose is a carrot, they should have an image of a real carrot in front of them as they work.

Teacher's Notes: _____

_____

_____

_____

39. Tiny Still-Life

Note: Students each get a small piece of base material (4x4 in.) that is available. (cardboard, foamcore, wood...) then glue on 6 objects from a pile of provided "scraps." These then become the basis for a drawing or painting.

Name _____ Gr. ____ Pd. ____

Do a sketch of your small collection of objects but make it fill this page.

Lower Elementary:
Pre-make some small collections of objects for students, or let them use collections made by older students. They should draw and make their picture larger than the actual objects on drawing paper. They need not sketch first.

Elementary:
Students should complete a sketch before working on final paper. They can bring in small objects from home as homework to be added into small collections. Objects should be fairly simple for this grade level.

Middle School:
Same as above, but objects can be slightly more challenging to draw. The addition of patterned items can help in this regard. Consider the use of oil pastels and watercolor. Some tutorials for media can be found here: www.goo.gl/kbEUsj

High School:
Students should sketch as above, working on more detailed items. Add some selections of patterned paper to the mix of potential supplies to raise the level of difficulty. It is helpful if students bring in small trinkets to add to their collections so they have a more personal connection to their work.

Extension:
Working in a paint media, working larger, taking time for details, textures, and patterns will also extend this project.

Advanced Extension:
Students should create their own miniature collections of objects to draw. Incorporate patterned pieces as well as reflective ones (foil/metal/glass). Encourage the use of a more challenging media like oil pastels or watercolors.

Teacher's Notes: _____

_____

_____

_____

40. White On White

Name _____ **Gr.** ____ **Pd.** ____

Create a sketch of an environment, a place you have been before or want to go to someday. Some places might be a desert, a forest, underwater, outer space, a cave, beach, or the mountains. There are many other possibilities.

Lower Elementary:
Place a large piece of paper in the front of the class. Choose an environment for students to focus on like a park, underwater, or the beach. Give students a sheet of white paper and have them cut out something for the scene. Each student cuts out their shape or object to be added to the scene to be displayed. Place pieces of cardboard under objects to make them pop-out. A scissor tutorial can be found here: https://goo.gl/ymZqQ8

Elementary:
Students could work as above making a single scene, or break into groups to make several scenes. Demonstrate how to add pieces to the larger display. A Glue tutorial can be found here: https://goo.gl/7n7JAN

Middle School:
Same as above, students can work in groups, or use the sketch page to work individually. See tutorials noted above for both glue and scissor use.

High School:
Students should sketch before working on individual scenes. If possible, they may be able to look up environments and create resources to work from. They should be encouraged to add textures to their papers by crumpling, cutting, scoring, or poking the paper. Review cutting and gluing expectations. Show them to be mindful of wasting paper, and to cut from the edges, not the middle.

Extension:
Adding detail, textures, and working larger can extend this project to a full week.

Advanced Extension:
Students could create a self-portrait or still life just from white paper.

Teacher's Notes: _____

_____

_____

_____

41. The Anatomy Of A Cartoon

Use skeletons on next page as reference images for students.

Cut these into 4 pieces and use as reference images for students.

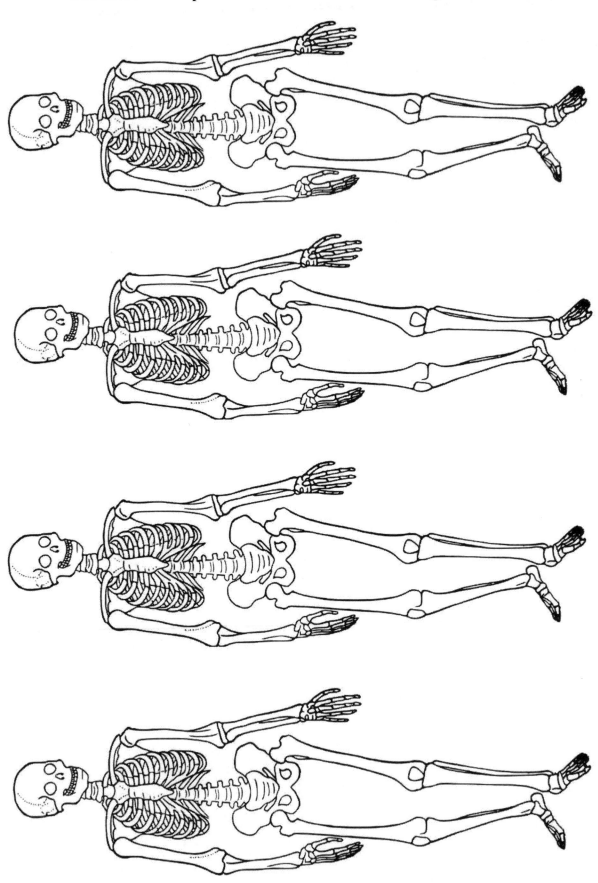

Name _____ **Gr.** ____ **Pd.** ____

Draw your favorite cartoon, and then show what their skeleton might look like. If you draw the cartoon very lightly, you can draw the skeleton inside.

Lower Elementary:
It may be helpful to have the contours of some characters available for students to choose from. Then they can draw in the bones. If they finish too early, coloring inside can lengthen the lesson to a full class period, or have a few extra characters for students to draw from.

Elementary:
Students should complete a sketch before working on final paper. Try to have students draw the shape of the character, then do a heavy outline of the contours (silhouette) with a permanent marker. Having some favorite characters, as reference may be helpful. The full lesson is detailed here: https://goo.gl/z2eQhi

Middle School:
Same as above, but encourage detailed contours. Students could print out their characters to full-page size and transfer the silhouette onto final paper. This video shows how to transfer an image: https://goo.gl/u8NZmb

High School:
Students should sketch as above, using more detail, and even shading in the skeleton. They could create a background as well to show where that character is usually seen. Some media tutorials can be found here: goo.gl/kbEUsj

Extension:
Adding more detail, working larger, completing more than one character, or having a more detailed background, can extend this project to a full week.

Advanced Extension:
Students could find a famous image from art history, realistic to abstract, and recreate the work with skeletons for main characters. Abstract works pose the most challenge and could be the subject for this project. Cubism and Surrealism may be good genres to explore for this.

Teacher's Notes: _____

_____

_____

42. Comic Book Covers

Your work should include:
Foreground
Middle ground
Background
Overlap

Name _____ Gr. ____ Pd. ____

Sketch a comic book cover below. Include a title, subtitle, logo, and main action. Try to show depth with a background, stuff in the middle, and overlap with something up front. (Foreground, middle-ground, and background)

Lower Elementary:
Students can do a drawing of themselves as a superhero or super villain. They should draw themselves doing something amazing they wish they could do, like fly, be super-strong, super-fast, magic, etc. Have a discussion before drawing of what superpowers they wish they had.

Elementary:
Similar to the above, students should discuss the superpower they wish they had. They should complete a sketch in the form of a comic book cover showing themselves as a hero or villain. Drawing tutorials here: www.goo.gl/kbEUsj

Middle School:
Students explore the idea of parody creating a comic book cover that puts 2 unusual characters together (like Godzilla & Spongebob) or a book that makes fun of a popular character (Hatman instead of Batman, Star Wreck instead of Star Trek) or create an original character of their own design.

High School:
Students should work as above but include more detail in the background, textures, layer colors, include shadows, more overlap, and create a better sense of depth. Drawing tutorials here: www.goo.gl/kbEUsj

Extension:
Students could make more detailed sketches and incorporate a critique of sketches for peer review before working on their final project.

Advanced Extension:
Students could create a movie poster parody. They can research a popular movie they like or one they hated, and make a re-creation of it as a larger illustration. Note the details that make a movie poster different than a comic book cover.

Teacher's Notes: _____

_____

_____

_____

43. The Non-Art Cartoon

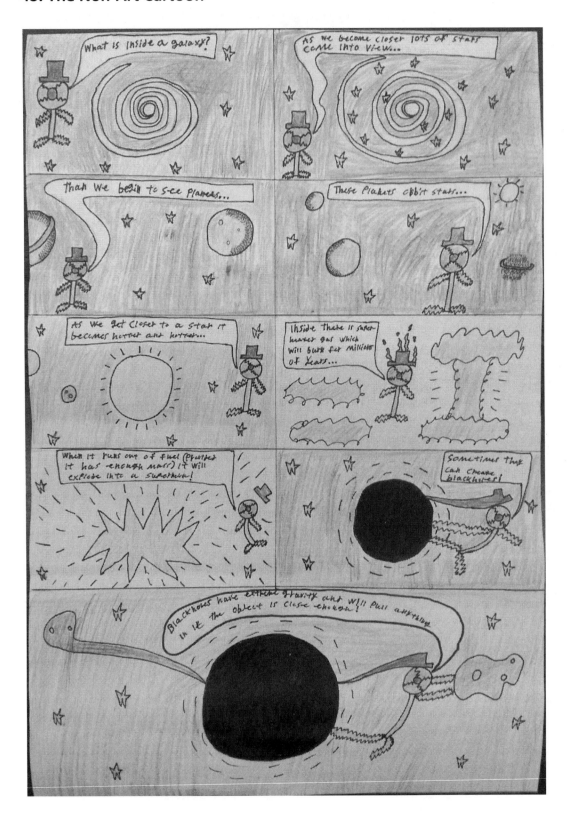

Name _____ **Gr.** ____ **Pd.** ____

Other than art, what is something you know a lot about? _____
Sketch a comic strip below that tells a short story or teaches others about your subject. It does not have to be funny, but should inform/teach the reader.

Lower Elementary:
Ask students and create a list of things they know how to do. (Make a sandwich, tie their shoes, take care of a dog, etc.) They should fold drawing paper 2x so it has 4 parts/panels, then draw a cartoon that shows them doing that activity.

Elementary:
Similar to above, students sketch out their skill or process in the form of a cartoon. It should be kept short, between 4 and 8 panels. They can include text that helps teach that skill to others.

Middle School:
Similar to above, students instead focus on a non-art skill they know well and create a comic strip that teaches about that skill. It can be playing a certain video game, how to fix something, or what they know about from another class, like cell division, photosynthesis, etc. Some tutorials can be found here: goo.gl/kbEUsj

High School:
Students discuss the subject, other than art, in which they are most successful. They pick a topic they can explain and illustrate, then create a comic strip to teach that information. They can make cartoons that could be used later to teach lower elementary students. Partnering with another department may be helpful in this.

Extension:
Adding details like backgrounds, textures, measured comic strip panels, and detailed color can extend this project.

Advanced Extension:
Students could partner with an elementary teacher, find a topic that instructor covers in their classes with students, and create a specific art/comic based visual to help teach or present that information.

Teacher's Notes: _____

_____

_____

_____

44. Paper Engineering

Paper engineering challenges are meant to be completed in one class period. Many examples can be found on the internet. Use the supplies available to you. These are some challenges that have been used successfully. If large paper (18x24 in.) is not available, multiple sheets of copy paper can work as well. These are usually done in small teams of 4. Offering some small reward can make the challenge fun.

1. Using 4 sheets of large paper (18x24 in.), 2 yards of masking tape, and scissors, students create the tallest tower possible. Towers should be free-standing (not lean on anything) but can be taped to the floor. Allow time to judge, clean up, and recycle materials.

2. Using 50 sheets of copy paper, 10 yards of masking tape, and scissors, make a stand more than 8 inches tall that a student can stand on. (Student testing the structure should hold onto something as they step up, so they do not fall.) Using an old hard-cover book on top of the structure can help create an even step, and can even be incorporated into the structure. Allow time to judge, clean up, and recycle materials.

Alternately, instead of having a student stand on the structure, textbooks can be piled on top to see how many the structure can hold.

3. Using 4 sheets of large paper (18x24 in.), 2 yards of masking tape, and scissors, students create a structure that extends from a flat wall. It cannot touch anything other than the wall. The structure (arm) that extends the furthest from the wall is the winner. Allow time to judge, clean up, and recycle materials.

4. Using 50 sheets of copy paper, 10 yards of masking tape, and scissors, make a bridge that spans between 2 tables, 12 to 18 inches apart. Test the bridge with weights (Books or other items) to see which holds the most weight at the time of collapse. Alternately, students could use glue and popsicle sticks. Allow time to judge, clean up, and recycle materials.

5. Using 50 sheets of copy paper, 10 yards of masking tape, 4 rubber bands, and scissors, make a catapult or mechanism that can toss a crumpled or folded piece of paper the furthest from a set starting point. Allow time to judge, clean up, and recycle materials.

Lower Elementary:
The paper tower is the easiest challenge for students. If they are unable to work in teams, give each student 10 pieces of copy paper and about 1 yard of tape to use. Scissors are optional.

Elementary:
Students should take 5 minutes to plan with their team before working. They should divide work up deciding who will do the cutting and assembly. For an additional challenge, you can require students work in absolute silence, only writing notes or using hand signals to build. If groups are too rambunctious, then working individually as suggested for the lower elementary level may be helpful.

Middle School:
Students should work in teams to complete a given challenge. They should sketch and plan for 5 minutes before building, but time this accurately. You can have them build in silence or not. Allow for enough time to judge their work.

High School:
Students should sketch as above with any of the challenges. If possible, the exercise can be repeated a second time after students research other similar challenges via the internet. This will improve their work and make for more structurally sound structures on a second try. Compare and contrast the results.

Extension:
Doing a different challenge each day will extend this project. Working with wood and glue will also take more time and effort. See advanced option below.

Advanced Extension:
Using a half or full ream of copy paper (500 sheets) and 1 bottle of glue, students could create a chair (individually or in teams) that could hold the weight of a person. They should sketch and plan before construction. Making paper into tubes will be helpful advice. Adding a research component may be helpful.

Teacher's Notes: _____

_____

_____

45. My Tiny Bedroom

Name _____ **Gr.** ____ **Pd.** ____

Sketch an object below, pretend it is hollow, and re-draw your bedroom inside that object. Choose something related to what you enjoy, collect, or use on a regular basis as the shape. (Stuffed animal, teapot, basketball, sport shoe, etc.)

Name _____ **Gr.** ____ **Pd.** ____

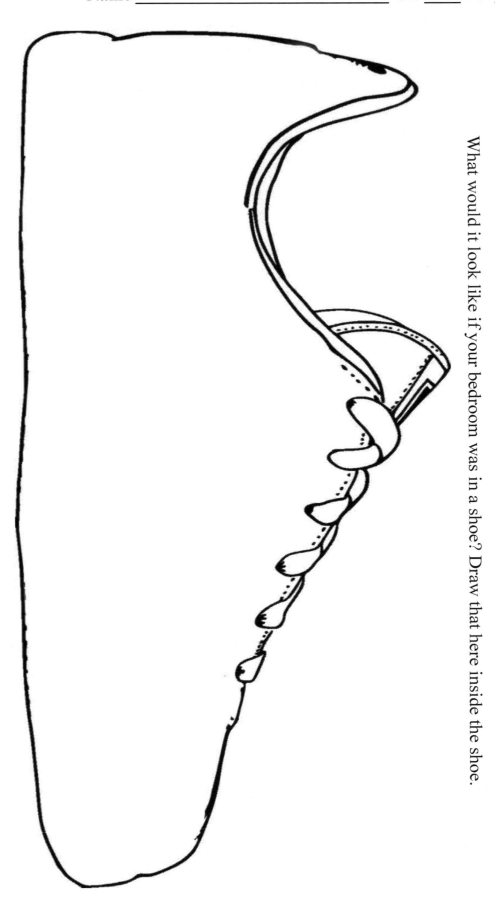

What would it look like if your bedroom was in a shoe? Draw that here inside the shoe.

Lower Elementary:
Students draw directly on their drawing paper and do not need to sketch. Create a list of objects that is familiar to students and will work with this project. (stuffed animal, basketball, shoe, etc.) Students do a drawing of their bedroom inside their object. It may be helpful to print out a few contour images, like the shoe on the previous page, and have students draw within the object.

Elementary:
Students should complete a sketch before working on final paper. These students can choose their own object, create a contour drawing, and add their bedroom. They should consider the things that are in their bedroom now. If they share a bedroom, they can make this one all their own.

Middle School:
Same as above, have students work in more detail and incorporate overlap for a sense of depth. They should incorporate color and textures.

High School:
Students should sketch as above, including overlap, foreground, middle-ground, and background. They should include patterns, layered colors, textures, and even shadows as they work.

Extension:
Adding more detail, pushing the idea of shadow, working larger can extend this.

Advanced Extension:
Students could create an actual environment within a container of some sort: box, flower pot, lunchbox, etc. They can construct items from supplies suggested by the teacher below. (Clay, paper, plaster, wood, etc.) They could also do this project as a collage unit, cutting and pasting images from home decor magazines.

Teacher's Notes: _____

_____

_____

_____

46. Weird Holiday Cards

Name _____ Gr. ____ Pd. ____

This is a list of real but weird holidays. Design a card for a holiday on the back of this paper. You can even fold this paper 2x to make it into a small practice card.

What holiday did you pick? _____

Weird but real holidays...

1-Jan	Polar Bear Plunge Day
2-Jan	Buffet Day
3-Jan	Festival of Sleep Day
4-Jan	Trivia Day
5-Jan	Bird Day
6-Jan	Bean Day
7-Jan	Old Rock Day
9-Jan	Word Nerd Day
17-Jan	Kid Inventors' Day
19-Jan	Popcorn Day
20-Jan	Penguin Awareness Day
21-Jan	Squirrel Appreciation Day
22-Jan	Hot Sauce Day
27-Jan	Chocolate Cake Day
29-Jan	Puzzle Day
3-Feb	Carrot Cake Day
4-Feb	Eat Ice Cream Breakfast Day
4-Feb	Thank Your Mailman Day
9-Feb	Toothache Day
9-Feb	Bagel and Lox Day
10-Feb	Umbrella Day
11-Feb	Make a Friend Day
14-Feb	Ferris Wheel Day
14-Feb	Library Lovers Day
17-Feb	Act of Kindness Day
19-Feb	Chocolate Mint Day
24-Feb	Tortilla Chip Day
25-Feb	Sword Swallowers Day
26-Feb	Pistachio Day
26-Feb	Tell a Fairy Tale Day
2-Mar	Old Stuff Day
6-Mar	Dentist's Day
10-Mar	Mario Day
11-Mar	Oatmeal Nut Waffle Day
13-Mar	Napping Day
14-Mar	Pi Day
16-Mar	Incredible Kid Day
20-Mar	World Storytelling Day
22-Mar	International Goof Off Day
23-Mar	Puppy Day
24-Mar	Chocolate Raisins Day
25-Mar	Waffle Day
25-Mar	Tolkien Reading Day
30-Mar	Take a Walk in the Park Day
1-Apr	Fun at Work Day
3-Apr	World Party Day
4-Apr	Tell a Lie Day
7-Apr	Walk to Work Day
10-Apr	Siblings Day
11-Apr	Be Kind to Lawyers Day
11-Apr	Barbershop Quartet Day
12-Apr	Grilled Cheese Day
13-Apr	Scrabble Day
14-Apr	Look up the Sky Day
16-Apr	Wear Pajamas to Work Day
17-Apr	Haiku Poetry Day
23-Apr	Take a Chance Day
26-Apr	Pretzel Day
27-Apr	Pinhole Photography Day
29-Apr	Astronomy Day
29-Apr	Zipper Day
30-Apr	Honesty Day
1-May	Batman Day
4-May	Star Wars Day
5-May	Space Day
6-May	Herb Day
6-May	Free Comic Book Day
6-May	Beverage Day
9-May	Europe Day
9-May	Lost Sock Memorial Day
1-Jun	Say Something Nice Day
2-Jun	Leave the Office Early Day
2-Jun	National Doughnut Day
4-Jun	Hug Your Cat Day
6-Jun	Drive-In Movie Day
7-Jun	VCR Day
8-Jun	Best Friends Day
9-Jun	Donald Duck Day
10-Jun	Iced Tea Day
11-Jun	Corn on the Cob Day
12-Jun	Red Rose Day
15-Jun	Nature Photography Day
17-Jun	World Juggling Day
17-Jun	Eat Your Vegetables Day
18-Jun	International Picnic Day
22-Jun	Onion Ring Day
24-Jun	Swim a Lap Day
26-Jun	Chocolate Pudding Day
29-Jun	Camera Day
30-Jun	Meteor Watch Day
1-Jul	International Joke Day
2-Jul	World UFO Day
3-Jul	Compliment Your Mirror Day
8-Jul	Video Games Day
9-Jul	Sugar Cookie Day
10-Jul	Teddy Bears' Picnic Day
15-Jul	Gummi Worm Day
19-Jul	Stick Out Your Tongue Day
24-Jul	Cousins Day
26-Jul	Uncle and Aunt Day
28-Jul	Milk Chocolate Day
29-Jul	Lasagna Day
30-Jul	National Cheesecake Day
1-Aug	Girlfriend's Day
2-Aug	Ice Cream Sandwich Day
3-Aug	Watermelon Day
5-Aug	Work Like a Dog Day
6-Aug	Sisters' Day
9-Aug	Book Lovers Day
3-Sep	Skyscraper Day
5-Sep	Cheese Pizza Day
8-Sep	Pardon Day
9-Sep	Teddy Bear Day
11-Sep	Make Your Bed Day
12-Sep	Chocolate Milkshake Day
15-Sep	Make a Hat Day
17-Sep	Country Music Day
18-Sep	Rice Krispie Treat Day
19-Sep	National Gymnastics Day
21-Sep	Miniature Golf Day
22-Sep	Hobbit Day
23-Sep	Checkers Day
25-Sep	Comic Book Day
4-Oct	Taco Day
6-Oct	Mad Hatter Day
12-Oct	Old Farmers Day
16-Oct	Dictionary Day
20-Oct	International Sloth Day
21-Oct	Count your Buttons Day
26-Oct	Howl at the Moon Day
28-Oct	International Animation Day
29-Oct	Internet Day
30-Oct	Candy Corn Day
31-Oct	Magic Day
1-Nov	Author's Day
2-Nov	Men Make Dinner Day
3-Nov	Sandwich Day
4-Nov	Common Sense Day
5-Nov	Zero Tasking Day
5-Dec	Day of the Ninja
6-Dec	Microwave Oven Day
8-Dec	Time Traveler Pretend Day
12-Dec	Gingerbread House Day
14-Dec	Monkey Day
19-Dec	Ugly Sweater Day
24-Dec	Eggnog Day
26-Dec	Thank You Note Day
28-Dec	Card Playing Day
31-Dec	Make Up Your Mind Day

Lower Elementary:
Choose 3 or 4 holidays for students to select from, or make up a funny but fake holiday for them to focus on. Students fold paper in half and create a card. They should color in. If spelling is an issue, write the text where they can see and copy.

Elementary:
Students should complete a sketch before working on final paper. They should share their sketch with a neighbor and seek advice on how to improve their work. They can fold drawing paper to make their final card. If thicker paper is available, it may be helpful to use. Media tutorials can be found here: www.goo.gl/kbEUsj

Middle School:
Same as above, students should sketch, share their results, seek feedback and then work on final paper. They should consider a background for their main image and work very neatly with coloring, layering colors if they can.

High School:
Students should sketch as above, including a background for their image with a sense of space. Incorporate foreground, middle-ground, and background in their illustration. They should include patterns, layered colors, textures, and even shadows in their work.

Extension:
Working in pen and ink with watercolors can be more challenging. Creating a few cards, and focusing on details can extend this project.

Advanced Extension:
Students could create cards for a special school function, school fundraiser, or event to be copied and used by the school. They could create art invitations for a special exhibition of their work with details inside on dates, times, and location.

Teacher's Notes: _____

_____

_____

_____

47. School Service Project: Awareness

Name _____ Gr. ____ Pd. ____

Write a famous quote about diversity: (www.brainyquote.com/topics/diversity)

_____

_____

_____

Design a poster to help educate and bring attention to the issue in a positive way.

Name _____ Gr. ____ Pd. ____

Sample Poster

AUTISM

Students with Autism are in our school and community. Words like "Retard" are hurtful, mean and intolerant.

FACTS:

- Autism is a neurological disorder characterized by impaired social interaction and communication.

- 1 in every 150 children is diagnosed with autism.

- The cause is currently unknown but does have a genetic link.

We could learn a lot from crayons; some are sharp, some are pretty, some are dull, some have weird names, and all are different colors....but they all exist very nicely in the same box.

Poster by students of _____ School Art Department

Lower Elementary:
Use this quote in the center of a large paper and have students create illustrations to add to the paper. "We could learn a lot from crayons; some are sharp, some are pretty, some are dull, while others bright, some have weird names, but they all have learned to live together in the same box." — Robert Fulghum

Elementary:
Using the same quote as above, students create their own poster to illustrate the quote. Have a discussion about what the quote means before sketching, and include the quote within the work. The teacher can provide printed copies of the quote to be glued onto posters or they can be hand-written.

Middle School:
Provide a list of many quotes about diversity for students to pick from or let them search for a quote to use. Many are here: www.brainyquote.com/topics/diversity Students sketch an image that includes the quote to promote diversity and acceptance in the school.

High School:
(See Poster Sample) Students can work in teams to research and create a poster about a social issue or specific population in the school that should be addressed or better understood. It is important for the instructor to be sure messages stay positive, thoughtful, and helpful.

Extension:
Working large, doing careful research, and using color can help extend this lesson.

Advanced Extension:
Students could create their own individual posters from either idea posted above.

Teacher's Notes: _____

_____

_____

_____

48. Blown Watercolors

Alternate project with blown watercolors

Lower Elementary:
Using straws, students blow small watercolor puddles of paint that branch and make trees. Do a demonstration with students gathered around you. It may be helpful to limit students to just brown. Markers can be used after to add themselves, leaves, and animals to their work.

Elementary:
Students can use 3 or 4 colors and create blown splatters with watercolor puddles. Video here of someone using the technique: https://goo.gl/4YGnjk Similar to the underwater sample image, students re-imagine the splatters as coral, seaweed, and sea creatures, adding details with marker or pen. Having photo samples of fish and sea animals will help.

Middle School:
Students can create self-portraits without hair, then add the hair with the watercolors dripped on and then blown. They can draw themselves with unusual expressions so that the wild hair looks more expressive. They should choose colors they feel are expressive of their personality. https://goo.gl/7PQ26Q

High School:
Students should sketch and practice before working on their final self-portrait.

Extension:
Encourage students to use a variety of colors. Consider the use of a pattern on their shirts, adding color to the eyes, and other elements can enhance the work.

Advanced Extension:
Students should experiment with the technique with watercolor and inks over 2 days. They should share after each session what they have learned or discovered, demonstrating for others to make clear what they did. Then create a work of art that uses these techniques independently.

Teacher's Notes: _____

_____

_____

49. Monograms & Letters

Name _____ **Gr.** ____ **Pd.** ____

Make a fancy sketch of your name initial. Include images of things that will show off your personality, likes, and what you enjoy doing.

Lower Elementary:
Students draw a block letter of their initial large and in the middle of their paper. Students draw themselves sitting on the letter, and put things in the letter that they like. Making a list may be helpful in generating ideas. (Food, games, cartoons, etc.) This tutorial will help for block lettering https://goo.gl/Hj8X7n

Elementary:
Students should complete a sketch before working on final paper with their initials. They can do both letters or just 1. Decorate around the letter(s) with images that will show off your personality, likes, and what they enjoy doing.

Middle School:
Students should sketch before working but make their letter more decorative. They should complete their work with background elements, and details that show off their personality and likes. Sample images based on the art in "The Book of Kells" can be found here and shared with students https://goo.gl/LDkH9R

High School:
Students should sketch as above, working with detailed letters and supporting images. They should include areas of pattern, layer colors, and include a background that helps illustrate their personality. See the link above.

Extension:
Students could work larger, or in a more challenging media like pen, ink, and watercolors. They could alternatively create a letter for the initial(s) of an historical figure with images that reflect that person's life.

Advanced Extension:
Students could create the initials of a famous artist in history, and use images that reflect that artists style and life within the initial. They could also create their own faux parchment paper by soaking paper in a coffee.

Teacher's Notes: _____

_____

_____

50. Poem Illustration

Illustration of a stanza of the poem, *The Jabberwocky* by Lewis Carroll

This image was created with a single continuous line.

Name _____ Gr. ____ Pd. ____

Pick 1 stanza from this poem to illustrate on the back of this paper.

Jabberwocky by Lewis Carroll (1871)

'Twas brillig, and the slithy toves
Did gyre and gimble in the wabe:
All mimsy were the borogoves,
And the mome raths outgrabe.

"Beware the Jabberwock, my son!
The jaws that bite, the claws that catch!
Beware the Jubjub bird, and shun
The frumious Bandersnatch!"

He took his vorpal sword in hand;
Long time the manxome foe he sought—
So rested he by the Tumtum tree
And stood awhile in thought.

And, as in uffish thought he stood,
The Jabberwock, with eyes of flame,
Came whiffling through the tulgey wood,
And burbled as it came!

One, two! One, two! And through and through
The vorpal blade went snicker-snack!
He left it dead, and with its head
He went galumphing back.

"And hast thou slain the Jabberwock?
Come to my arms, my beamish boy!
O frabjous day! Callooh! Callay!"
He chortled in his joy.

'Twas brillig, and the slithy toves
Did gyre and gimble in the wabe:
All mimsy were the borogoves,
And the mome raths outgrabe.

What's going on in this poem?

The first and last stanza create a scene where the story takes place. What do these words make you think the scene looks like? Swampy, grassy, desert?

A father warns his son about 3 creatures. The author often puts words together to make new words, like "Frumious" = Furious + Dangerous?

The son has a special sword and sits by a unique tree waiting for the monster. Or is it just a boy with a stick and a great imagination? Could be either.

The monster has eyes like fire, makes a wiffling sound, and burbles. Is a burble and burp mixed with a gurgle? What might this monster look like?

The son kills the monster by chopping off its head! He is pretty happy he succeeded because he galumphed back home (Gallop + Jump?).

The father is happy the son is back and alive. Maybe he is playing along with the son's vivid imagination. Either way, it works with this poem.

The last stanza is the same as the first. Instead of an introduction, this becomes the closure.

Lower Elementary:
Read students an age appropriate poem or short story without sharing the illustrations. Poems by Shel Silverstein are good to work with: https://goo.gl/6w8D4V   Have students reflect on the reading, and do a drawing of their favorite part of the story. They should share their work with the class.

Elementary:
Same as above, but have students create a sketch before working. They should share their sketch with a peer for suggestions and then work on final paper.

Middle School:
These students may be old enough to try and decipher the Jabberwocky poem. A rough translation has been written next to the poem to help. They should sketch on the back of the poem paper and illustrate one stanza. If they include the text and divide stanzas between classmates, the whole poem can be displayed in school. If the poem is too challenging, pick something else.

High School:
Students should sketch as above before working. The sample image was created with a single line that was used loosely to create an illustration. Students could practice this technique (continuous line drawing) to create their own illustrations. Media tutorials can be found here: goo.gl/kbEUsj

Extension:
Having students create a sketch and then a painting that includes the text can extend this project. Work should be displayed in the school or library.

Advanced Extension:
Students could find their own inspirational poems, or write an original poem, then create a work of art that includes the poem and illustrates it.

Teacher's Notes: _____

_____

_____

_____

Critique with sample:

Critique of artwork is by __Vincent van Gogh__   Title/Description: ____Starry Night_____

From 1 (not showing) to 10 (very strong) rate the following parts of the project:

Neatness = __8__,   Completeness = __9__,   Originality = __10__,   Following directions = __10*__

What art element is the strongest in this project? _Line seems to be an important art element in this work_

Evidence: __All major parts seem to have an outline, and all the paint is done in short line brush strokes.__

What art principle is strongest in this project? __Many are, but movement stands out for me.__

Evidence: __The sky seems to swirl, the hills are like churning waves, stars seem to twinkle,__

What is most successful about this project? ___*Van Gogh set out to try and do a painting of a night sky from observation, so he met his goal. It is a very original idea.___

Besides completeness, what could be improved upon in this project: _There are some small portions of the canvas showing between paint strokes. Coloring the canvas first may have hid this._

What can you say about the artist based on their artwork (Be positive): _I feel that the artist wants us to pay attention to the beauty around us, maybe we don't pay attention enough._

Name _____ Gr. _____ Pd. _____

Critique of artwork is by _____ Title/Description: _____

From 1 (not showing) to 10 (very strong) rate the following parts of the project:

Neatness = _____, Completeness = _____, Originality = _____, Following directions = _____

What art element is the strongest in this project? _____

Evidence: _____

What art principal is strongest in this project? _____

Evidence: _____

What is most successful about this project? _____

_____

Besides completeness, what could be improved upon in this project: _____

_____

What can you infer about the artist based on their artwork (Be positive): _____

_____

Critique of artwork is by _____ Title/Description: _____

From 1 (not showing) to 10 (very strong) rate the following parts of the project:

Neatness = _____, Completeness = _____, Originality = _____, Following directions = _____

What art element is the strongest in this project? _____

Evidence: _____

What art principal is strongest in this project? _____

Evidence: _____

What is most successful about this project? _____

_____

Besides completeness, what could be improved upon in this project: _____

_____

What can you infer about the artist based on their artwork (Be positive): _____

_____

Name _____ Gr. ____ Pd. ____

Universal Art Project Rubric

	Criteria				Points
	100	90	80	70 - 65	0/F
Elements & Principles of Design	Planned carefully, made sketches, and showed an advanced awareness of the elements and principles of design. Student went above and beyond expectations	The artwork shows that the student applied the principles of design while using one or more elements effectively. Student met expectations.	The student did the assignment adequately, yet shows a lack of planning and/or little evidence that an overall composition was planned.	The assignment was turned in, but showed little evidence of any understanding of the elements and principles of art; No evidence of planning. Student did the minimum of work required.	____
Craftsmanship & Neatness	All aspects of the artwork were considered and patiently completed. The finished product is a result of careful meticulous planning. The craftsmanship is outstanding. Project is pristine and well kept.	With a little more effort in finishing techniques, the artwork could be outstanding. Overall, the project is clean and without major defects like folds or rips.	The student showed average craftsmanship; adequate, but not as good as previous work or a bit careless. Minor folds or stray marks may be present.	Craftsmanship was poor, lack of pride in finished artwork. Little evidence of effort and/or a lack of understanding. Includes obvious deficits like folds, rips, and/or stray marks.	____
Time & Management	Class time was used wisely. Much time and effort went into the planning and design of the artwork. Student was actively engaged and self motivated.	Class time was used wisely. Some time and effort went into the planning and design of the artwork. Mostly independently motivated.	Some class time was used wisely. Some time and effort went into the planning and design of the artwork. Student was sometimes distracted.	Class time was not used wisely. Little or no effort went into the artwork. Often reminded to stay on task.	____
Execution, Originality, & Uniqueness	The artwork was successfully executed from concept to completion, with a novel and original approach.	The artwork was successfully executed from concept to completion. Unique & original with some evidence from samples.	The artwork was moderately successful from concept to completion. Includes some unique aspects.	The artwork was begun, but never completed. What work was done was highly derivative of the samples or other student's work.	____
Requirements & Depth	All requirements are met and exceeded. Intense exploration of subject & techniques.	All requirements are met. Subject and media were well explored.	One requirement was not met completely. Subject or technique was not fully explored.	More than one requirement was not met. Little depth of subject and technique.	____

Comments:

Grade ____

Name _____ Gr. ____ Pd. ____

Student: If you did more or less than the expectations please explain in writing. If you met the expectation, circle it. If a requirement is poor or missing, mark it as **deficient**.

	Criteria			Points
	20/100 Advanced	18/90 Expected	16/80 Approached	Deficient
Elements & Principles of Design		The artwork shows that the student applied the required principles of design while using one or more elements effectively. Student met expectations.		____
Craftsmanship & Neatness		Overall, the project is clean and without major defects like folds or rips. With a little more effort in finishing techniques, the artwork could be outstanding.		____
Time & Management		Class time was used wisely. Time and effort went into the planning and design of the artwork. Mostly independently motivated.		____
Execution, Originality, & Uniqueness		The artwork was successfully executed from concept to completion. It is fairly unique & original with some evidence from samples or peers.		____
Requirements & Depth		All requirements are met. Subject and media were explored as required. Some personal connection or point of view is evident.		____
Comments				Grade ____

Assessment: **Graded by both the teacher and the student. Only the teacher's grade counts, but if there is a difference between the assessments, this can be discussed.**

Project Title _____ Date Complete _____

Short Description: _____

Assess a grade of "A, B, C, D or F." You may add + or – if you feel the need.

Student Assessment Below   **Teacher Assessment Below.**

Neatness ____	Neatness ____		
Completeness ____	Completeness ____		
Originality ____	Originality ____		
Following Directions ____	Following Directions ____	____	
Meeting Project Goals ____	Meeting Project Goals ____	Recorded Grade	

Project Title _____ Date Complete _____

Short Description: _____

Assess a grade of "A, B, C, D or F." You may add + or – if you feel the need.

Student Assessment Below   **Teacher Assessment Below.**

- Neatness ____
- Completeness ____
- Originality ____
- Following Directions ____
- Meeting Project Goals ____

(Teacher side, same items)   Recorded Grade ____

Project Title _____ Date Complete _____

Short Description: _____

Assess a grade of "A, B, C, D or F." You may add + or – if you feel the need.

Student Assessment Below   **Teacher Assessment Below.**

- Neatness ____
- Completeness ____
- Originality ____
- Following Directions ____
- Meeting Project Goals ____

(Teacher side, same items)   Recorded Grade ____

Project Title _____ Date Complete _____

Short Description: _____

Assess a grade of "A, B, C, D or F." You may add + or – if you feel the need.

Student Assessment Below   **Teacher Assessment Below.**

- Neatness ____
- Completeness ____
- Originality ____
- Following Directions ____
- Meeting Project Goals ____

(Teacher side, same items)   Recorded Grade ____

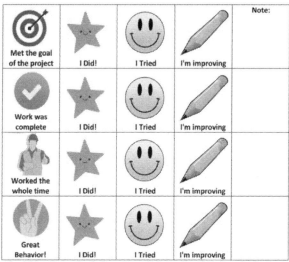

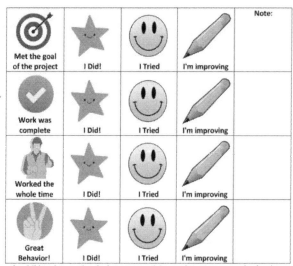

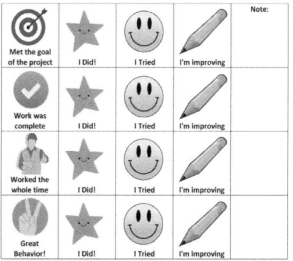

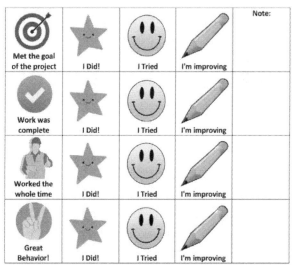

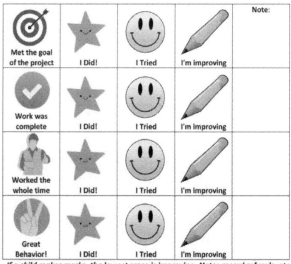

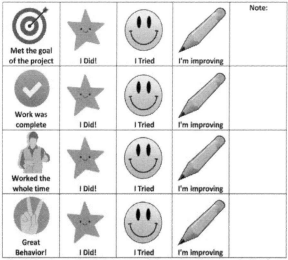

For more art award winning art education resources please visit:

**www.FirehousePublications.com
or
www.ArtEdGuru.com**

Made in the USA
Columbia, SC
02 February 2020